building for the GOSPEL

'This is a splendid resource for anyone considering a building project of some kind at church. Completely packed with spiritual wisdom, practical advice, and worked examples. Julia Cameron has done us a great service!'

Lee Gatiss
Director of Church Society

'Absolutely essential for anyone becoming involved in a church building or restoration project. A church is about something far more profound than bricks and mortar.'

Joseph Kelly
Editor, Church Building magazine

building for the GOSPEL

A handbook for the visionary and the terrified

J E M CAMERON

Building for the Gospel
A handbook for the visionary and the terrified

First published by the Church Society 2017

The original story of St Nicholas, Sevenoaks, on which the idea for this book is based, was first published in 1997. Completely revised and updated 2007. Second complete revision and updating 2017.

Published for Church Society by Lost Coin Books, London
email: lostcoinbooks@gmail.com
web: www.lostcoinbooks.com

LOST COIN

Church Society
Ground Floor, Centre Block
Hille Business Estate, 132 St Albans Road
Watford WD24 4AE, UK
Tel +44 (0)1923 255410
www.churchsociety.org
admin@churchsociety.org

ISBN: 9781784982706

Printed in the UK

Contents

With thankfulness to God for the lives of

Canon Miles Thomson, Tony and Eve Wilmot,

and others in and behind these stories who

have now joined the great cloud of witnesses.

Author's note

I am grateful for the time of all those with whom I have talked or corresponded, and to Lee Gatiss for the kind interest he showed when he heard this little handbook was to be updated. Our hope is that it will serve in three ways, namely:

- to help churches already launching into building projects
- to encourage churches which are holding back
- to give ideas to churches not yet thinking about possibilities

I trust the accounts touched on here will bring inspiration, and strengthen the nerve of many other churches. Have a look at the websites of the churches featured or join them on a Sunday if you are in the area.

I send these stories on their way with prayer.

JEMC
Oxford

'From beginning to end, it has been as much a project about faith as it has been about design, funding, building and use.'

Andrew Butcher

St John the Baptist Church, Burford

'We have experienced God's power financially and practically; and in the peace, unity and generosity that have marked the whole project.'

Daniel Grimwade

Dewsbury Evangelical Church

'We saw our building project just as one little milestone in one small corner of God's great gospel story. We were a part of something so much bigger.'

Paul Couchman

Cornerstone Church, Nottingham

Royalties from the sale of this book have been assigned to the building fund at St Ebbe's Church, Oxford.

Start here

Churches in many towns and cities have struggled with decisions about their buildings over the past 30 years; even more will do so over the next 20 years. Church leaders have understandably seen reticence, even fear, when ideas of building projects have first been aired because they are so expensive.

For everyone finance is a major consideration. High property prices mean high mortgage repayments for those who can raise a deposit, and high rents for those who can't. Christian parents find themselves pulled in several directions as their children want the same things their friends have; for single people the pressures are different, but they are no less real. It is part of our culture to live at the edge of our means, or slightly beyond that, so financial pressure has become part of life.

What can we 'afford' to give? How can we be sure that others will also give sacrificially, so as to make our own giving worthwhile? We all know that a church is more than a building, so do we really need better buildings anyway? Some questions are focused on the project itself, and others spring from an understandable desire to protect our own or our families' financial interests from what could be perceived as a threat. It is good to ask questions.

Plans for a building project emerge out of prayerful reflection and discussion, which can last many months, even several years. Feasibility studies have to be taken seriously during this process. They cost money, and some people naturally find it hard to give money before they know that the project will definitely move forward. There are questions to ask about the all-week-round life of the buildings, how they are used, and how they could be used; and what the implications of the new space would mean for the level of staffing. If the church itself is to seat more people, what knock-on effect does that have on car parking, or kitchen facilities, or ancillary hall space? How will the extra numbers be cared for pastorally? How would that affect the budget for staffing?

Decisions are made differently in churches, depending on the church tradition; there is no right or wrong way of reaching a final decision. In some churches the elders or church council[1] take responsibility for such decisions; in others they have to gain acceptance from a specified majority of church members. In every church the leaders will bring the same hope: that the outcome of discussions will seem, to borrow the words of the apostles in Acts 15, 'good to the Holy Spirit and to us'; that there will be a real sense of the Lord at work, bringing a unified decision.

This doesn't mean everyone will be persuaded to the same extent, or at the same time; some may take months or longer to come to that point. The project can begin only when the 'Must we?' has turned into a clear 'We must!' It is at this point that the long and daunting journey begins.

Here we draw on the stories of several churches. Since the previous edition, new illustrations have been added, from both rural and urban contexts, as more churches have moved along the challenging and costly road.

The way forward will depend on a range of local factors, and decisions need to be well-informed. Take, for example, the church in Cuckfield, East Sussex. Previous extensions had filled the whole footprint of the site, yet continuing growth meant they now had too small a build-

1 For this book to be useful across different church traditions, denominational terms have been avoided where possible.

ing, with unsatisfactory access, no circulation space, and too few toilets. However the leadership felt they were not yet ready to bring plans to the congregation. It was a further two years before leaders felt they had a clear-enough picture of what was needed. Over this time, a new question came to mind. If people were coming from outside the village, could a daughter church be a preferable option? This would bring a further set of questions, but could not be quickly dismissed. However as houses were built and sold, and the growth of the congregation tracked, it was clear that new members were in fact local. The leaders now sensed with confidence that the Lord's direction was to rebuild on the church car park, which was a field, large enough to provide for a new church facility and for car parking space.

Other churches have had very different stories to tell, as they have endeavoured to serve in preservation areas, in city contexts, among students and among the urban poor. In each place, the church has been willing to set out on an adventure of faith to serve the Lord's purpose in this generation, as our predecessors did in theirs.

Milestones of remembrance

There is something biblical about a stone of remembrance. God urged the Israelites to 'remember' and to tell their children of his acts. Many church leaders who have gone through building projects will have stories to tell of particular meetings, or conversations, or emails, or calls, where it became clear that the Lord was in the decision, and that he would undertake if the leaders showed courage, and moved forward.

I recall the discussions at St Ebbe's Church, Oxford from 2013, when the council began to reflect seriously on the need for extra capacity. There was a sense of dissatisfaction with the building, but not a unified sense of what to do. In the Autumn of 2015 it was suddenly clear that everyone was persuaded. One member of the council articulated what others were feeling after. 'I now see the need,' she said. 'I've changed my mind.' In everyone around the room the Holy Spirit had been working gradually, over the previous year and more. It was not until the following meeting that the chairman called a vote. But, looking back, the unanimous decision had already been made.[2]

The limited St Ebbe's building was being worked hard, as were the church apprentices, a team of new graduates. Meals were cooked in a small kitchen for large groups several evenings each week, for students and young professionals who met for Bible study around tables. These heavy circular tables then had to be wheeled behind the organ for the church to be set up for daytime activities. Servant-heartedness was high on the Profile for the apprentices; that and braun. While lack of space had never been allowed to hinder the full midweek diary, greater space would free up a considerable number of set-up and set-down hours in the week.

Meanwhile in the north of England, the building used by Dewsbury Evangelical Church on Crackenedge Lane, was becoming increasingly full.[3] Its lack of facilities were limiting the gospel work which the church wanted to do in the town. There is a large, influential teaching Mosque in the heart of Savile Town—an area referred to as the 'Islamic Republic of Dewsbury'. Fifty percent of Dewsbury's population under 19 is of Asian origin. Many townspeople are employed in the local bed factories. So Dewsbury has two of the hardest groups of people to reach with the gospel—Muslims and white manual workers.

There had been regular stock-takes of buildings which were becoming available to rent or buy in the vicinity. Now it was urgent to find somewhere bigger, and in 2009 the church moved into the Scout Cen-

---

2 See Chapter 5. This was for the addition of a gallery on three sides of the church. By March 2016 a proposal was taken to the congregation, which, if the money could be raised, would incorporate the purchase of the adjoining rectory from the diocese, and the purchase of the leasehold on 'a nearby building'. Six months later, after sensitive negotiations, that building could be identified as the nightclub a few yards away. The rectory, and the leasehold on the nightclub, were both to be purchased by a newly-formed Trust.

3 Dewsbury Evangelical Church was founded in 1972. The town, situated just south of Leeds, has, in the words of co-pastor, Daniel Grimwade, 'made the news for all the wrong reasons. The leader of the 7/7 bombers lived here (2005); and in 2008 it was on the front pages with the kidnapping of Shannon Matthews.'

tre in Heckmondwike, west of Dewsbury, at the foot of the Pennines. This gave ideal space with all the necessary facilities and it was cheap to rent. However it was three miles from Dewsbury town centre, so not ideal. The leaders couldn't allow the members to become comfortable there, and it was decided that a more proactive approach was needed to find a new home. Given the large Asian community in Dewsbury, a new base would need to be in a neutral area, not regarded as primarily 'Asian' or 'white'. Over the course of a few weeks, there was clear agreement that a building would have to be purchased.

Daniel Grimwade explains:

> *We looked at several options that required a huge amount of work, and were very likely beyond our reach financially, then a building became available in Central Street. God was answering our prayers, and this created a buzz. Here was somewhere that met all our needs, in terms of overall size, number of rooms, price, location, and a manageable amount of work needed, which could be done in a few months. The church could see the vision, and wanted to step forward in faith. Before work started in Central Street, we held a service there (with the congregation bringing their garden chairs). This created a real sense of expectation.*
>
> *In many ways it is a mystery where all the money came from for the improvements and refurbishment, as the church had already given sacrificially for the building's purchase. We highlighted the need, and prayed, and the money came in—much of it from within our membership. It was kick-started by a £25,000 donation which had to be partly used to buy new chairs. The donor wanted no involvement in the choice of chair, but just wanted to make sure we had new chairs! Following that, gifts rolled in week after week, such that we were able to give the green light to new packages of work every week without delaying the programme. It was a remarkable and exciting journey as God provided for us, just at the right time. In the end we did everything on our list and had a fully-functioning building by the time we moved in, at the beginning of March 2014.*

Cornerstone Church in Nottingham had been meeting in the city's Bluecoat School for 15 years, having outgrown its previous building. This school allowed for growth, and while it had at the outset been regarded as temporary, the church had become settled there. A building fund had been set up using the proceeds of the sale of its previous building but few, if any, people were giving to it on a regular basis.

At the Annual General Meeting in April 2008, the church leaders brought a proposal to promote more serious giving to the building fund. It was a motion in principle and not detail, and it was carried overwhelmingly. One possibility, which had been on the table for over two years, was to explore a partnership with the school, as part of the school's ambitious redevelopment programme. The church would build on school land, while the school could make use of the church building. It was an unusual proposal, but it seemed as if this could be the way ahead.

Later that same month Peter Lewis, the Pastor, was invited to meet with the school's new chair of governors. A surprise was to come when she said the school would not accommodate the arrangement. The school had been accepted for the government's 'Building Schools for the Future' arrangement, and this could not allow such a partnership.

Action was required quickly as building work at the school would commence in January 2010, and the church was required to vacate by September 2009.

Peter talked with the Elders, who greeted the news with a strange sense of relief, for while it was unexpected, it brought clarity. The following Sunday, everyone received a letter from Peter as they came into church.

> *We can either hear this as a rumble of thunder or the crack of the starting pistol,' he wrote. 'We have been on the starting block for two and a half years now, waiting for clarity from the various authorities involved. We have been through the "Get on your marks, get set.... get on your marks, get set.... get on your marks, get set"... waiting in vain for the "Go!" Now we have it.*

He put to the church the vision of building for a hundred years.

> *That is not extravagant when you consider the nature of the city and its two universities, nor when you think that we have babies in the crèche who may well be alive in a hundred years from now.*

He concluded:

> *The mountain rises far above us at the moment, but when we stand on its summit we shall sing to the glory of him who is greater than all the difficulties and who will fulfil his will in our lives.*
>
> *Yours in the love of Jesus,*
>
> *Peter*

The message from the school conveyed a clear message from God. Unintended by the governing body, it was to provide a stone of remembrance.

That Sunday the church organized the first of several weeks of prayer. They wanted to seek God's guidance on new premises. It would involve:

- Locating suitable land and acquiring planning permission
- Finding significant financial resources
- Keeping the church together after vacating the school building

Location was important. To move out of town would offer cheaper land, but, as Paul Couchman (building project manager) notes: 'We needed to be close to the city's universities and hospital as student accessibility had become a key factor of the church's growth and mission over several years.'

X

St Paul's & St George's Episcopal Church, Edinburgh is in York Place, close to the city centre. As with all city churches, many members are professionals, but there are crowds of students, a growing number of retired people, and some who are unemployed. Its large building drew fewer than twenty members in 1985. Today St Paul's and St George's is a wonderful story of growth. Plans for a church plant in the city's expanding South East Wedge ran alongside the building project.[4] Total cost: close to £6m for a major refurbishment and additional Welcome Area, 2007.

Adventures of faith demand faith. And there can be times when that faith is not easy to maintain. The Christian life is often described as 'a fight of faith'. From the inside it can seem more like 'a fight for faith'.

In 2000, when Miles Thomson, Rector of Sevenoaks, looked back five years to the completion of the Undercroft beneath St Nicholas, he wrote: 'Time and time again, turning to Nehemiah steadied our nerve and kept us to our vision.[5] He continued:

> *We had, from the outset, committed ourselves not only to build a building, but to build a people; to build a church family who live under the authority of God's Word in God's world. It is still our prayer to keep on growing in faith as well as increasing in numbers, and to keep on training people in service, both in this country and overseas.*
>
> *We want to see more people finding a personal faith in Christ, and growing in their knowledge and love of him. We want to see more people taking Scripture as their guide at school or college, and in business, commerce, education or health; more going into pastoral ministry; more working to build God's church worldwide. We thank God for all the ways we are already seeing this happen; we pray he will enable us to carry on building for the gospel.* [6]

The St Nicholas, Sevenoaks story goes back the furthest of all those in this book, so has had the longest time to bear fruit. Its building is now used seven days a week, and has two morning congregations. Further, two new churches: The 4 o'clock Church and Grace Church are now established in the town. As others in the book will testify, building proj-

4 This was forward-thinking. Shawfair (not at that stage named), the new town to be created just outside Edinburgh's municipal boundary, will have some 4,000 homes.

5 See Appendix 2

6 A few months later Miles Thomson was diagnosed as suffering from a brain tumour. He went to be with Christ on Boxing Day 2000. The growth of the work in St Nicholas is testimony to the Lord answering this prayer.

ects have a lasting effect on the lives of the church family. They help to change mindsets and forge a deeper quality of Christian discipleship. In the words of Angus MacLeay, Rector of St Nicholas, Sevenoaks from 2001, 'Somehow, sacrificial giving is now part of the life-blood of the church, and I am sure much of this was learnt through the exciting but difficult years of the building project.' St Nick's later partnered with a church in inner-city Liverpool, led by a former member of its youth group. Over the years, with its larger member-base and, as Angus said, more-practised givers, St Nick's has sent out and funded a steady stream of younger men and women into gospel ministry in the UK and in several countries overseas, extending the ripples of influence.

May God give us that desire for 'more', so characteristic of the Apostle Paul, in all our churches.

Chapter 1

Bricks, mortar and the gospel of Christ

All building projects have the same end in view: better facilities for teaching, training, fellowship, evangelism, serving the community. This is the essence of church life—growth in depth, in numbers, in effectiveness, in service, all for the glory of Christ.

We are getting much more audacious about building projects. Forty years ago it seemed daring to spend a few thousand pounds on carpeting a church and replacing pews with chairs. And now we see a project in Edinburgh which cost nearly £6m. To compare the number of zeros in those sums tells its own story.

While the expenditure has increased, the range of initiatives has also grown. Some churches have been built above shops; other churches meet in converted warehouses; a few have been designed in partnership with the local council or a local school. But the end is the same in each case: to provide a church building which is fitted to contemporary needs.

John Stott, the pastor theologian who was for many years Rector of All Souls, Langham Place, adjacent to the BBC in London's West End, summed up the needs of all human beings in three ways:

- everyone reaches for a transcendent presence outside the created universe
- everyone feels a need to matter in our digitalised and fragmented society

- everyone needs to know they belong when so little value is placed on family

If the first century Christian gospel is to relate to twenty-first century life, we must engage with people in these areas.[7] This book won't look at how we do that as a church, but at the kind of buildings we need to facilitate this. The two are closely connected. Our buildings need to be suited to our purposes on Sundays and for midweek events; but they are also the places where we can invite friends, and introduce them to the gospel in a range of ways, and equip Christians to be effective as the church at large: to shake salt and to shine light in our local community, through professional networks, and in public life.

Buildings can be a public proclamation of Christian belief in a pluralist and secular culture. Where the building draws many people, those who live or work in the area notice. We should not underestimate the value of presence.

Is it good stewardship?

We can naturally resent the need to spend money on bricks and mortar when the church is really about growing the Lord's people. Anglican church buildings don't belong to their members, so improving them can seem a bit like spending money on a house which you don't own. People may ask 'Isn't it better stewardship not to spend money like that?' Buildings belonging to a Free Church congregation may legally be owned by its members, but even so, shouldn't we give that money to world mission instead? Again, these are good questions.

In Scotland, some whole congregations have left the denomination, because of the way the Church of Scotland has departed from Scripture. Other evangelical churches have chosen to remain within the

7 Drawing from thinkers and writers including Mother Teresa, Woody Allen, Bertrand Russell, and columnists from *The Independent* and *The Economist*, he identifies (i) the quest for transcendence, (ii) the quest for significance, and (iii) the quest for community. See 'The Contemporary Christian' pp521ff in *The Essential John Stott*, (IVP, 1999).

denomination. To resolve to leave a denomination is a major decision, which can be taken only by the minister and elders of the church, who know the situation best. To engage with the pros and cons of such arguments is beyond the mandate of this book, nor would it be right to pass judgment on either way forward.[8] Will the Church of England become a place where evangelicals can no longer function freely? Much at the moment remains unknown. The Premises Development Group at St Ebbe's, Oxford needed to be clear with the congregation, many of whom do not have Anglican roots, exactly what the position was. So the last section of their briefing read:

> **We are committed to the Church of England**
> *We gladly affirm our commitment to the Church of England's doctrine, as expressed in Canon A5,[9] and its mission as a national church to seek to reach, pastor and serve the whole population. We are grateful for the many benefits of being members of the Church of England which include, among many things, the use of the Church building, garden and Rectory. We do not desire or plan to leave the Church of England and do not envisage circumstances in the foreseeable future when we would feel the need to do so.[10] However, we should recognise that there are some concerning trends which may make it difficult for evangelicals to function in the Church of England in the longer term. For this reason we would be wise to remember that any investment we make in the church property would be in buildings that we do not ourselves own.*

8 Where an Anglican parish church has an evangelical patronage, the current patrons are often able to ensure an evangelical succession. If the rector has freehold, the church council can be sure of retaining the same leadership until that person reaches the statutory age for retirement; but the next rector will not have freehold. (General Synod 2005 voted to abolish freehold succession.) So decisions have to be made on the strength of what can be known, and in faith.

9 'The doctrine of the Church of England is grounded in the holy Scriptures, and in such teachings of the ancient Fathers and Councils of the Church as are agreeable to the said Scriptures. In particular such doctrine is to be found in the Thirty-nine Articles of Religion, the Book of Common Prayer, and the Ordinal.'

10 Vaughan Roberts, current Rector of St Ebbe's, has freehold, which will last until he is 70, God willing, but not pass to his successor.

Chapter 2

The Vision, and the people to make it happen

Whether you are in a market town or in a university town, in a farming community or in a multi-cultural city, your church acts as a beacon for the gospel in that context. Building projects vary enormously in shape, size, and cost, but acting as that beacon is the central theme of each, and the unifying theme of all.

The story of St Nicholas, Sevenoaks forms the backbone to what follows, with illustrations added from other churches. God deals differently with different people in different places, but the common thread of Christians 'working together with him' (2 Corinthians 6:1) is clear to discern through all the accounts. However the journeys taken have not always been easy.

Early on in the process, each of the churches formulated its own vision statement to help focus the minds of the church family on the central reasons for the project.[11] Drawing up such a statement helps a whole church family to re-focus on what is essential. The wording varied in each case, but the message was the same.

John Bridger of Reigate Baptist circulated a thoughtful paper in preparation for the church's decision entitled 'Church planting as an

11 I have drawn from different churches' stories along the way. All of the churches produced similar literature, but I refer only to one example at each stage for easier flow.

option for growth.'[12]

St Paul's & St George's, Edinburgh communicated their vision with great effectiveness through FAQs (Frequently Asked Questions) on the website. The touchstone question came first.

> **Q:** *'How do the building plans fit with the vision?'*
>
> **A:** *Our mission is to bring people and God together; our vision is to build a Christ-centred, culturally-relevant, biblical community, worshipping and serving in the centre of Edinburgh; our strategy is to make, mature and mobilize people as disciples of Christ. [The answer then continued with specific references to plans.]*

To make disciples, to nurture them towards maturity in Christ, and to equip them to serve him in strengthening his church—what a wonderful threefold purpose for buildings to serve. Are they fit for that purpose, now and looking into the future? This is the key issue for churches. To look at options and discuss them openly among the leadership and membership is a necessary foundation for the process.

Those closely involved in these projects have vivid memories of times when it seemed plain that God was on their side, and of other times when the discouragement of fellow church members was all they could hear; fellow believers who wanted the whole project forgotten for any one of a host of reasons. Because those church leaders pressed on, their stories—and the buildings which now stand—can exhort other churches for years to come.

Hudson Taylor, the chemist's son from Barnsley in West Yorkshire who became a pioneer missionary to China, once said: 'There are three

12 Here he outlines the basic needs of a church most likely to succeed in a major project. The list begins with being conservative theologically, having strong pastoral leadership and includes a commitment to prayer, well-applied Bible teaching, and generosity in giving. There will be a range of views among evangelicals as to how some areas are best worked out, but the paper, which finishes with advice for any churches considering a plant, is stimulating for everyone.

stages in any great work of God. Impossible. Difficult. Done!'[13] At the moment your building project may still loom as impossible.

Getting the right people

Appointing the right people to responsibilities is key to effective working in any setting. Tony Wilmot gave a major thrust to the St Nicholas, Sevenoaks Undercroft.[14] He brought a mix of spiritual aspiration, shrewd judgment and professional experience. He was a man who looked at what was, and saw what could be.

The world over, able people are often the busiest, and church leaders can feel reticent about approaching those who are already heavily committed. On the basis that people have to make their own decisions before God, the policy Miles Thomson adopted in Sevenoaks was to invite those with suitable gifts and qualities to consider taking on responsibilities. He then trusted their judgment as to what they could manage. By approaching them, he was not putting any pressure on them. He knew they would reflect on the matter carefully and with prayer, and he felt they were the best-placed to make the decision. Miles would write rather than putting people on the spot. Receiving a letter in the post gave time for reflection. Emails in a crowded inbox can quickly disappear from view; or if they are read in the melée of a busy morning at work, it is hardly the context for careful and prayerful thought.

Church members themselves will be able to take the project to a certain level, but the church will then have to engage professional architects and an experienced Project Director. The Project Director may be found from within the church family, or move house to become part of the church family.

13 Founder in 1865 of the China Inland Mission, now OMF International.

14 Tony Wilmot, already retired, had spent much of his life in Africa as a colonial servant and businessman. He was a moving spirit behind the founding of several IFES movements in African nations.

Project Directors

The wide-ranging role of Project Director will draw on every transferable skill a person can bring. This role is central to the smooth-running of all aspects of the project: liaison with planning authorities and ecclesiastical authorities; interface with the work forces; and the flow of communication internally and externally. A critical part of the job is organizational ability. They will come from different backgrounds. Emma Vardy came to St Paul's and St George's, Edinburgh from a background in freelance work. As an event manager she had arranged professional conferences, concerts, and other events; she also brought experience in fundraising. Brigadier Ian Dobbie, Project Director at St Nicholas, Sevenoaks, had served in the Royal Engineers and as an instructor at Sandhurst, and had held office in the Directorate of Manning in the Ministry of Defence, and as deputy chief of staff of an armoured division.

The ethos of a project like this is very particular. Not only is it not-for-profit like any charitable venture, but it is for the glory of God. To be able to draw on the right people, who have skills and experience suffused by spiritual judgment, is all-important. For this reason, church members with professional backgrounds in finance, communications and construction are often brought onto a building committee so their expert advice can be pressed into service throughout the project.

How was the right combination of talent and judgment found in St Andrew's, Leyland?[15] In God's providence, Steve Watson, an architect from Manchester, had moved into the town and joined the church two years before the Vision Builders project was launched. It soon became clear that he could serve as its consultant architect. He would sit in the church building to let the ambience sink in while he thought through

15 St Andrew's Church, Leyland dates back to the 12th century and serves a pleasant Lancashire town of 38,000 people where the main industry has been vehicle design since 1896. The first major reordering (the Vision Builders initiative) was completed in 1999 at a cost of £500,000. The second phase began in 2005. This included more refurbishment, and a new venture: an evangelistic café-style church plant, meeting at 5pm each Sunday in the local high school.

ways of bringing the vision to its most effective and aesthetic reality. The church council accepted the tender from a local firm, Marland Bros, and Jack Rimmer, its managing director and a longstanding church member, took personal responsibility for the project.

In 2010 Daniel Grimwade became co-pastor of Dewsbury Evangelical Church, alongside Graham Heaps. Daniel had previously worked as a consulting engineer in the building industry, so brought experience in project management. He oversaw the whole project from finding the building to working with the design team and builders. Having two pastors working together meant only one was 'distracted' by the building project. To prevent Daniel from being totally absorbed, a project co-ordinator was employed for a few months to relieve him of the sundry pieces of admin that come up in a project like this.

Two months before the project at Cornerstone Church, Nottingham got underway, Paul Couchman had taken redundancy from a bank in the city. He met up with one of the leadership team, to pray and discuss the future. They read Psalm 143, which summed up the state of his heart, especially verses 7-10.

So when the church needed a new building, Paul was able to give time to the search. As the job description came together for a Project Manager to oversee this work, it became clear that Paul was the man for the job. He understood the church's vision for the building and would be able to communicate it to architects, lawyers, builders, surveyors, planners, engineers, and designers. He could ensure decisions were made in a timely manner to keep the project moving forward, and communicate what was happening to the church. While he had no construction experience, he had transferable skills in every other area.

Establishing a steering committee was an early priority for Paul. This consisted of one of the elders, the church manager, and two or three church members who had relevant work experience. This steering group would give needed encouragement and support to Paul throughout the project.

In Burford, it was decided not to appoint a Project Director, but to draw on skills in the congregation. Some of those with needed skills were semi-retired; others still in full-time work. Their backgrounds included accountancy, legal practice, project management in engineering, and senior leadership of a company. Alongside their professional backgrounds, they brought soft experience of proven inter-personal skills, successful project management, a knowledge of fund-raising and ability in handling complex organizational structures. The final building contract was for circa £3m. Given the size of the project and the complexities of the building site, it was essential that the church appoint an architect, quantity surveyor, and consultant engineers. These appointments proved invaluable and cost effective.[16]

Some churches appoint a separate treasurer for the building project; others combine the role with that of the church treasurer. The faith of the treasurer will be contagious in council meetings, and in the church as a whole. Andrew Butcher says of Burford, 'We were blessed in having a church treasurer who wanted to spend money. He recognised that the project is a 'faith' project, and encouraged the church to keep moving forward. When we had completed the scheme design (RIBA Stage D), we decided to proceed quickly onto the detail design (Stage E) even though we did not have enough money to go out to tender. The needed funds became available by the time we had completed Stage E. I think many treasurers would have been more cautious in moving forward at that point.'

Natural gifts and abilities, transferable experience, together with a shared commitment to the cause of the gospel—these will all be found in those who are leading church building projects. One other facet is also needed, as we see in the next chapter: patient resolve.

16 The church followed the standard stages set out by the Royal Institute of British Architects (RIBA), available as a free download (ribaplanofwork.com). Recommended payment terms are typically calculated as a percentage of building contract costs.

Chapter 3

Gaining permission is not always easy

As many readers will know from experience, householders can find themselves running into difficulties if they want to build an extension, or change the use of their home to incorporate a small business. We have words like 'red tape' and 'bureaucracy' in our language only because we need them! But for all the difficulties a home-owner may encounter, the matter is much more complex for a church.

As we have noted, Anglican church buildings do not belong to the congregation; church councils often have no jurisdiction over them, though they are bound to keep them in good order. Permission to alter an Anglican building can be given only by the chancellor of the diocese on behalf of the Bishop. The chancellor himself is a layman, usually a former lawyer or judge. Outside courts have had this kind of jurisdiction over church buildings and their burial grounds for several hundred years. For independent churches, the decisions can usually be reached by the congregation, generally requiring a high percentage attendance at the meeting and a high percentage (if not unanimous) vote of those present for significant changes. All these decisions are then subject to town or city planning authorities in the same way that any other applications are.

Gaining permission can be a testing time, and those who are driving the planning applications need the prayerful support of the rest of the church. The processes can be long and complicated and in seeking an acceptable way forward church councils are rightly concerned to find solutions—and means of reaching them—which do not alienate local residents or businesses, and which commend the gospel rather than raise antagonism.

Obstacles, obstacles

St John the Evangelist, Carlisle, encountered particular problems from a local Councillor with their project at nearby St Andrews Botcherby. He moved quickly to have the building listed, which in the end worked to the church's advantage, as it enabled the church to claim back VAT.

Steve Donald, the vicar, explains: 'The Councillor twice opposed the plan to install a glazed door at the front of the church, to replace two wooden doors at the sides. The side doors were of particular difficulty in funerals, with coffins having to be dropped to almost vertical level, and walked around a forty-five degree angle.'

'After the Councillor's objections, the local planning officers visited the site, and were won over. The Councillor had argued for a plan which would have altered the historic fabric of the building; now the glazed door, which retained a sympathy for the design, was agreed.'

'Following the council planning meeting at which the decision was taken, one member of the council said he liked my "sermon". (I had explained that the glazed door was fitting because the gospel involves removing barriers, and is about welcoming people.) Prayer, patience and persistence, whilst seeking to be gracious and winsome, were the secrets to our success in going forward.'

For the church in Cuckfield, obstructions lasted for more than ten years. During this time the church employed three architects. The first became unavailable after a time; the second proved too expensive. Both had produced schemes that the planners dismissed on what seemed flimsy grounds.[17] The planners' main objection was that the church car park on which the new building would stand, lay outside the village

17 But permission had already been granted for sports buildings, standing on land designated as an area of outstanding natural beauty.

boundary. As the car park did not intrude into the green belt between Cuckfield and the next conurbation, Haywards Heath, it should not have posed any difficulty. The planning system seemed to be designed around a 'tick-box culture', and this took patience to break through. It seemed to count for little that there had been a chapel on the site since 1772! While there was a degree of opposition from a few individuals, the church had clear support from the community generally, as from the Parish Council. It was the third architect who would produce a plan which would find favour with the town planners.

St John the Baptist church lies in the town of Burford,[18] much of which is a conservation area with many buildings remaining from medieval times. From the start, the plan to create a more useful facility for the church out of Warwick Hall, adjacent to the churchyard, was widely recognised as 'big, bold and scary'. (This phrase, coined at the church weekend away, was readily adopted as encapsulating exactly what the plan would mean.) It would incur significant cost, and it could succeed only if God were behind it.

St John the Baptist owned Warwick Hall, which was used by both the church and the town. To be more useful, it needed to be re-thought. It comprised two large meeting areas with a kitchen, toilet facilities, and garden. Access was not easy, down two steep, uneven steps. The heating system was inefficient, and bookings for events were dropping off.

Its use by the town meant that the church initiative to improve it would be seen as a way of genuinely serving the needs of the community. The redevelopment would provide an original, improved hall, a new larger hall seating up to 200, three other new meeting rooms, and ancillary facilities including an office. All ground floor facilities would be on one level. Given the setting in this Cotswold town, it was essential that the building be attractive as well as functional.

The main part of Warwick Hall is a Grade II listed building, sitting

18 Burford is a small town dating back to Saxon times, set in the heart of the Cotswolds.

adjacent to the Grade I listed church and grounds.[19] When the church sent a formal petition requesting a faculty from the Diocese to enable the work to be done, two local residents raised a formal objection, rallying support from half a dozen others. While the complainants were few, this was to lead to what could have been a deeply disheartening disruption. In July 2014, the Rector, Richard Coombs found himself facing a Consistory Court hearing, held in the church, flanked by a Church Warden, the Chairman of the Finance Committee, the architect, and the Town Mayor.

The court is presided over by the Chancellor of the Diocese in gown and wig. Some 80 or 90 people from the church attended as observers, but the proceedings weren't easy to follow because much of the evidence from both sides was presented in a bundle of papers lodged with the court beforehand. The bundles comprised over 800 pages and if the evidence had not been contested, it was accepted as read by the court. It was an intense day, from 10.00am to 4.00pm with an hour's break for lunch.

The Chancellor's judgment, an 18-page report, was delivered the following month. The process inevitably delayed the start of the building work and added significantly to the costs.

But, as with the Councillor in Carlisle, the opposition of some was used by the Lord for good. The Chancellor's judgment was wholly in favour of the church. One difficulty had been the ownership of the wall between the churchyard and Warwick Hall, and permission to create a new entrance into the Hall through it. The PCC had assumed the wall was shared. However, digging back into antiquity proved this not to be the case. It was originally the wall of a separate building and therefore outside the churchyard. It did not need the permission of the diocese for change now or in the future. Part of the opponents' case was that the redeveloped hall should be used only for 'ecclesiastical' purposes. 'We believe they were trying to restrict social and perhaps noisy or crowded

19 Simon Jenkins lists the church in his *England's Thousand Best Churches*, giving it five stars, one of only 18 in the country.

uses,' explained Andrew Butcher. The Chancellor agreed that the Hall should be used for 'the whole mission of the church', defined in section 2(1) of the 1956 Measure as its 'pastoral, evangelistic, social and ecumenical' mission, which covers any activities it may want to host.

In working through the difficulties the church family was encouraged by several events which could have happened only if God had ordained them.

- A generous gift was received for an architect to prepare plans for the PCC and Project Team.
- The 25-year-lease on Warwick Hall, granted to the Town Council in 1987 expired in April 2012, at exactly the right time for the PCC to have freedom to develop it.

'These helped us believe that the Lord was driving this project forward and so increased our faith to strive ahead.' The Lord's hand was clear in (i) the willingness of all statutory planning authorities to allow us to develop this sensitive site; (ii) the speed with which substantial funds were raised; (iii) the unanimous support in the church, and (iv) the range of skills and experiences within the church family and design team.' He added, 'It is a joy to see how some members have grown much in their faith through these times.'

In Leyland the Farington family, benefactors to the town of the lovely Worden Park, had a special interest in the church building. They had, generations earlier, paid for the Worden Chapel, set at the front of the nave. To keep this chapel in its original position would have given an asymmetric feel to the new interior of the church, and the church council applied for permission to move it further back. But the current generation of the family were naturally reluctant for changes to be made. The matter was taken to a Consistory Court, and the church lost its appeal. Eventually agreement was reached with the family and the chapel was moved back five feet. The Farington family's gift is part of the long St Andrew's story, and no one wants to edit out these significant contributions in history.

In Edinburgh, permission for work to begin in St Paul's & St George's was expected to take the statutory six to eight weeks, but this stretched to nine months. The church is a Grade A listed building and news of the plans was greeted with nervousness by Historic Scotland. This could have led to a great sense of frustration for the church family. However, Dave Richards, the rector, boldly encouraged the church to press on with its giving program, so that money given early could start to gain interest. These months were filled with much paper and millions of electrons as required information was gleaned and passed on; for most of this time there was little hard news to report Sunday by Sunday.

Dave, Emma, and the building committee had to accept the delays and pray for grace in all their dealings with those who were causing them. While it was generally assumed that permission would be granted, all who gave money at this stage were exercising believing faith. Eventually, with the support of the Scottish Executive, Edinburgh City Council approved the plans, and Historic Scotland's concerns were overruled. By the time the church moved out of its building, three quarters of the necessary funding had been pledged. The new building was finally opened in 2009.

For St Nicholas, Sevenoaks (or St Nick's as it is often known) the waiting period lasted much longer. It took thirty years to gain all necessary permissions for its Undercroft. The Sevenoaks Society, the Royal Fine Arts Commission and the Department for the Environment had each mobilized support against the church. Over this protracted period two different solutions to the accommodation problem were ventured but rejected. The level of antagonism grew so high at one stage that Michael Heseltine, then Secretary for the Environment, involved himself personally and ruled against the plans. St Nick's is a medieval parish church surrounded by a graveyard, set at the north end of a largely comfortable commuter town. It took nearly 30 years for building plans eventually to come to fruition.

The words 'but God' sum up much of what happened in Sevenoaks over the next few years, as he worked to change situations, and to change people's minds, in answer to prayer. The solution to gain eventual acceptance was to be much more radical. It might appear that the secular authorities overruled the plans in the interests of the publics they served. Perhaps the higher truth was simply: 'But God meant it for good'.

Chapter 4

Children's work

Spiritual and practical considerations tend to run in parallel; indeed the right spiritual solution will always prove to work at a practical level. One area in which this is often seen is how arrangements work for children's clubs on Sundays.

A large proportion of Christians are converted when they are young, through the influence of Sunday clubs, through school friends, camps or houseparties, through reading the Bible for themselves, or perhaps through a university mission. As people start work and take on mortgages, spiritual matters are often sidelined. There is no longer any social pressure to have a baby 'christened', so the first big opportunity for parents to be linked with a church can be when their children reach Sunday school age. Many parents still want their children to learn about God. They may feel inadequate themselves as teachers if they do not have a good grasp of the Christian faith. What they need is a church that will welcome the family, and make them feel at home.

Up and down the country we are seeing more and more churches with good premises taking creative initiatives in family evangelism during the week. Midweek clubs for pre-school children can be a highlight for mothers at home with their little ones, and for nannies or other carers. Here the children can play while parents and carers talk. Often there is some singing and a Bible story. The children enjoy learning the songs, and spiritual truths can start to seep in through the words. With such little biblical knowledge taught in schools, adults are likely to be as new to the Bible stories as the children. These midweek events can prove invaluable as bridges. They can spark off events for fathers who are at work during the week, through initiatives like 'Just Daddy and me' (where fathers are invited by their children to come on an occasional Saturday to see what the children are doing), or men's breakfasts, where friendships can be formed with church members.

Paul Batchelor, treasurer of the 'Building for the Gospel' project in Sevenoaks, was drawn back to church through its children's work. He and his wife, Janet, had both attended the University Church while students in Cambridge, but it was not until they started bringing their children to the Sunday school in Sevenoaks that they found personal faith in Christ. Paul Batchelor was at that time on the international management team of what is now PriceWaterhouseCoopers. Very soon after he came to faith, the then building fund treasurer resigned, and Paul was asked to replace him. 'I had a crowded diary, heavy travel commitments, and knew it could only bring more pressure. But after much discussion and prayer, Janet and I decided I had the needed skills and it was right for me to accept. For both of us it proved a faith-building exercise, and we were privileged to be part of it.'

It was the growing children's and youth work which gave particular impetus for the church in Burford. There was already a thriving weekly 'Rock-a-Tots' group, (essentially mothers and toddlers) which was providing an entry point for some to explore the Christian faith, or to be drawn into parenting classes. From here, they were then more able to join a small Bible study group. Some townspeople, and a few on the church fringe, felt that the building would become a white elephant if it were designed around the needs of the children's groups.

To win the trust of families, careful thought needs to go into the children's work. The location of the crèche and the Sunday clubs is important. Is the accommodation warm, safe, light? Will parents be able to leave the children and get into the service in good time or will they have to walk some distance from the crèche or Sunday clubs to the main church building and risk arriving late, and feeling conspicuous?

In St Ebbe's, as the numbers of families grew, the prams and buggies were making it impossible for people-traffic to flow through the very limited church centre. A gazebo was erected each week in the church garden to house the buggies, which solved that problem. But overcrowding in the limited meeting spaces needed more radical solutions.

Chapter 5

Looking at options

Jesus used a building project to help illustrate what it means to become a disciple. Just like people who are about to embark on a major construction, he said, anyone thinking hard about being a Christian also needs to count the cost.

> *Suppose one of you wants to build a tower. Will he not first sit down and estimate the cost, to see if he has enough money to complete it? For if he lays the foundation and is not able to finish it, everyone who sees it will ridicule him, saying, 'The fellow began to build and was not able to finish.'* (Luke 14:25-35)

Jesus knew people's hearts. He knew that matters which touch our bank accounts are taken very seriously. And that is why he chose the illustration.

For the church to look honestly at options, each has to be weighed carefully. Whatever the way ahead, the cost must be counted with care. A feasibility study will be needed, presenting the hard data of what things will mean in cash terms.

There are likely to be three main options. These of course will vary. A church with a small footprint, perhaps defined by the convergence of two roads, may have less choice as to how plans can proceed. But no church has fewer than two options, and most churches have three.

> **Option 1:** This is always the same. It is to do nothing. To proceed in this way is a real option, and needs to be set alongside the others as a possible choice. What are the benefits of doing nothing? What would be the longer-term costs?

It is critical for this option to be examined carefully as the discussion will determine much of the way a church proceeds.

While a cost/benefit analysis of any option can be handled on a flip chart at a church meeting, the benefits and deficits of the 'do nothing' option can also be discussed at home and with friends, for everyone knows the current buildings well. If there are problems about accommodation, this option would pass the problems on to those who followed. While it demands no courage or sacrificial giving, it offers no solution to pressing needs.

> **Option 2:** This is the relatively low-cost way forward. It will vary from church to church.
>
> **Option 3:** This is the visionary way forward. It will mean a level of sacrificial giving which will hurt everyone: the low earners, the middle earners, and the high earners.

St Ebbe's, Oxford was by 2012 holding four services on a Sunday.[20] It dates back to medieval times, now literally poised between town and gown, the Westgate shopping centre a few feet to the west and the back of Pembroke College to the east. The building is not large, so there are multiple services on a Sunday. Should a gallery be added? An obvious question first needed to be addressed; a variant on the 'do-nothing' option, which would save considerable time, resources, and inconvenience: Not all services were full, so could some people be persuaded to move from one service to another, to even-out the size of congregations, and still have extra space in all of them? This was not a disingenuous question. But even if people did move from one congregation to another, the capacity issue would be solved only in the short-term.

The parish includes a homeless shelter, council flats for elderly resi-

---

20 In 2001 St Ebbe's planted a congregation in Headington, a suburb in which the main campus of Oxford Brookes University is situated. Sixty people opted to join the plant. The aim was threefold: to start a distinctively Bible-teaching church in that area of East Oxford; to see gospel work progress among Brookes students; to clear space at central St Ebbe's for further numeric growth. The plant began with an evening service only, held in a school. In 2006 a Trust was established for the purchase of a building, in Lime Walk. This enabled, over time, better midweek outreach to families, groups for students and young people, and three Sunday services. St Ebbe's in Headington now supports its own mission partners.

dents, and homes for some of the neediest families in the county. Evangelistic events are held frequently to enable the church family to invite friends—elderly people, some vulnerable adults, as well as hundreds of students and under-35s. Numbers were continuing to grow; a full building could have offered a beguiling sense of satisfaction. But that was not how the Church leaders wanted it to be viewed. They urged that the hundreds on a Sunday be compared not with previous numbers, but with the many thousands in the city who had never heard the gospel. This was the background to the 2015 decision referred to previously.

It was agreed that information with costings would be necessary, for a sound judgment to be made. Over the course of another year or more, the St Ebbe's Premises Development Group (PDG) began to explore different scenarios. Still no decision had been made to move forward, and the 'do nothing' option had not been discarded.

Meetings brought many questions and the Council was roughly equally divided on preference. Should a gallery be built? Or an extension into the church garden? If either, what further ancillary space would be needed? With the help of an architect, the PDG then brought careful drawings and costings so the Council could weigh the benefits of how the work would be done, if it were to be done. It is a church Council which works hard at unity, and the rector and chairman were not rushing decisions. Unity came, as we saw earlier, in a decision to take Option 3.

In the case of St Nicholas, Sevenoaks, Option 3 was to dig a hall beneath the church. It meant spending a lot of money simply to explore its technical feasibility. In the 1990s no hall had ever been attempted beneath a medieval building anywhere in the world. It was, as the architect Robert Potter later described it, 'almost too challenging to do more than whisper'.

Let's think behind the scenes in Sevenoaks. There was an unavoidable question in the back of everyone's mind. 'What if exploratory digs show the project is not feasible?' Money was needed for the digs, and it could all come to nothing as the 14th century foundations might not allow a substructure. To brace a church for generous giving with a goal in sight is one thing; to ask people for significant giving when the goal is uncertain is another.

Christ Church in Dunstable was in a similar situation in 2000.[21] It needed money for a project which might not work out. The plan was to purchase The Plume of Feathers, an ancient coaching inn, well-known in the town, and just three doors away. This was a derelict Grade II listed building which dated back to the 1700s, and permission for change of use was by no means certain. Would members of the church family take a godly risk and make a blind investment? They did, and they kept giving as new problems kept being discovered. The inn had fallen into such disrepair that seven tonnes of rubbish needed to be removed from it. Refurbishment began late in 2003 and The Way, a Christian Community Centre for the town, was opened in October 2004. Thank God that members of Christ Church took that risk. Growth of The Way led to a second project: extending its own premises.

Some initial blind investment is almost always necessary. Similar circumstances (ie of requiring a substantial sum with no assurance of the project's success) could arise in any church. Perhaps a nearby building comes onto the market, as happened in Dunstable, and it needs to be purchased before permission for change of use is certain. Or adjacent land needs to be bought quickly before planning permission for an extension can be worked through.

Even if the church has land on which to build, or an asset like Warwick Hall, there can be a need for sometimes complex (and therefore expensive) plans, to submit to the town council or ecclesiastical bodies. Which church members will provide this money? It takes risky faith to sacrifice a family holiday or a change of car at such an early stage of a building project. No one doubts that.

Moving up the option scale

The original plans at St Andrew's, Leyland had been costed at £370,000.

21 At this stage it was still known as West Street Baptist, Dunstable

Steve Watson's advice to replace the church ceiling at the same time took the total to nearly £500,000. The future dreams adopted in 2005 included plans to take out the pews and replace them with chairs, and to install small TV screens below the galleries and a large plasma screen at the front of the nave. This plan would enable those without sight lines to see the preacher, and ensure that everyone could read words on a screen. But the screens alone would cost £16,000. Another major dream lay beyond that: to rebuild the large adjoining church hall, and to create a new role for the staff team—a leader for a 5pm café-style service. So substantially more money would be needed as time went on. Option 3 was being stretched; faith that God would provide needed to be stretched too.

With 80 members at a parish weekend away, the church still seemed full. Regular members had to be asked to meet in the church hall for the annual Remembrance service. A local soldier had died in Iraq and the church would be jam-packed on Remembrance Sunday for years to come. The Vision Builders were looking to God for further growth. How could they not grasp the opportunities he was giving? As we will learn, the church family accepted the challenge.

'We did it—you can too'

Being urged on by a church which has already been through similar difficulties can be a huge help. Linking with a church for prayer, partnership and encouragement can be a wonderful support. St Nicholas looked to All Souls, Langham Place in this way. Bishop Michael Baughen, its former rector, came down to St Nick's at a critical period, when it was vital that the whole church family gain ownership of the plans.

He related a story which gave heart:

> *'All site meetings at All Souls started with prayer. The workmen had felt uneasy about this in the first few weeks, and had perhaps been a little embarrassed. But they got used to it, and from time to time even asked the church to pray when they found something problematic. One afternoon the site manager asked for prayer as the local district inspector was being difficult. That evening at the church*

prayer meeting, the matter was again brought to the Lord; people didn't know what to ask, but were keenly aware that this man was causing problems. The next morning, news came that he would not be raising any more difficulties. He had been promoted!'

Michael Baughen then went to the question of money. Is it right for a church to spend so much on its buildings? He spoke perceptively. Some who ask this have genuine concerns, and need reassurance about the project. If they prefer to make a substantial gift to overseas work instead, they must feel free to do that. But it would not be right to think of a building project as 'spending money on ourselves'. It is 'spending money for Christ's Kingdom'. And as homes become more and more comfortable, it is appropriate to think of ambience for a church, too, so friends invited to church feel 'at home'. Churches, he added, will always testify that giving to a building project releases money for other things too, and general giving moves up significantly.

Bishop Michael also helped St Paul's & St George's. He had followed its story since 1985 when Roger Simpson became its vicar.[22] That year a church in Corstorphine, four miles west of Edinburgh city centre, had commissioned several of its members to help revive this large, empty church, and invited Roger to lead what was then essentially a church plant. Dave Richards knew of this link and invited the Bishop to preach one Sunday, and to meet with church leaders. Michael Baughen urged the church family in Edinburgh to look forward in confident hope, and to think of generations to come. Taking the congregation into Exodus 33 he exhorted them to plead just as Moses had: Lord, teach me your ways, and show me your glory.

Thinking of the generations to come, he would tell people of how it still gave him 'joy to see All Souls crowded, used and working, and to think of what it's done for hundreds and hundreds and *hundreds* of young people.'

---

22 Roger Simpson had served a curacy under Michael Baughen at All Souls. He is now Archbishop's Evangelist for the Northern Province.

Chapter 6

Believing God

First, a lesson from history on the adventure of faith. James Hudson Taylor founded the China Inland Mission (now OMF International) in 1865. He believed that 'God's work done in God's way will never lack supply'; and these words have strengthened many Christians in faith ventures ever since. Surely that 'supply' does not relate only to finance. It also applies to the spiritual, physical, and emotional resources people need to keep going if they are to finish the task. As Hudson Taylor prayed for new workers, he never imagined the way ahead would be trouble-free. His team of recruits in China, without any formal language training, was derided in the House of Commons as 'the pigtail mission'; and there was homesickness and lack of trust among those who found it difficult to accept Taylor's authority. Years later, just as he was to hand over office as general director of the mission, his chosen successor died—with over 50 other missionaries—in the Boxer uprising. Hudson Taylor's enduring faith was not born out of naïvety. OMF International celebrated its 150th anniversary in 2015.

For any church venturing out in faith, God is at work in people's lives—at times remarkably; at other times almost imperceptibly. Stick-ability is needed for a building project. From the first pledge day to moving back into the church could typically take as long as four years, and throughout this time the initial effort needs to be sustained.

How will local historians chronicle hopes and plans for your church in decades to come? That will depend on who writes the history. To onlookers, these projects consist only in bricks and mortar, permissions and contractors. But that leaves too much unsaid. The whole purpose is to create facilities to bring honour to Jesus Christ. They are spiritual projects, and can be truly perceived only with that purpose in view.

The Apostle Paul wrote to the Ephesians that God is 'able to do immeasurably more than all we can ask or imagine' (Ephesians 3:20-21). Bishop Michael Baughen had referred to this on his visit to St Nick's as a 'very major promise', and these rich verses were to prove a source of hope and stability throughout the whole process. The same verses were included at the end of a longer passage (verses 13-22) read by Steve Watson at the celebration service in St Andrew's, Leyland. If scripture is God's Word for his world for all time, and if it is true and sufficient, then we will be able to draw strength from it.

Reigate Baptist Church started life in a community centre on a large housing estate. The centre was, to quote John Bridger the pastor, 'completely unchurchy' (which was in its favour for drawing in new families) but it soon became too small. The church then moved to a local school hall. Through the five-year journey from the church's founding in 1995 to the opening of its current building, John Bridger turned over and over again to God's promise to the Israelites, as revealed in a dream to Nathan: 'I will provide a place for my people Israel and will plant them so that they can have a home of their own and no longer be disturbed' (2 Samuel 7:10).

The Lord brings sustenance through deepening our grasp of his character—the character of the One who is able to do more than all we ask or imagine—and through reminding us of his dealings in the past, which are recorded for our learning.

For St Paul's & St George's Church in Edinburgh, different verses had special significance. One was Joshua 3:4: 'Then you will know which way to go since you have never been this way before.' Following God often means stepping out into the unknown. Dave Richards preached a series of sermons on trusting God, and invited John Ortberg (author of *If you want to walk on the water, you need to get out of the boat*) to preach as part of that series on Jesus' invitation to trust him.

Rising costs

Even when the plans remain the same, rising costs are not unknown. As the cost rose for St Paul's & St George's, the church family turned to the life of Abraham who was promised a son when humanly speaking this was impossible. 'Yet he did not waver through unbelief regarding the promise of God, but was strengthened in his faith and gave glory to God, being fully persuaded that God had power to do what he had promised.' (Romans 4:20-21) As Emma Vardy explained, 'It challenged our ability and willingness to trust God despite current events.' If they had indeed discerned God's leading aright, then they must not falter now through fear or unbelief.

Bringing a new figure to a congregation is not easy when everyone's budget is tight. Daniel Grimwade explains the Dewsbury situation: 'As we had to make a fairly quick decision to buy the property we could not obtain detailed quotations for the work. Once the alterations were properly priced we found we needed significantly more than we had originally hoped. However, the Lord had already provided enough for us to press ahead with phase one, which would have allowed us to make the building usable. As this work was being done we defined phase two more exactly. As we did this, the Lord provided the funds. We were greatly encouraged by Ephesians 3:20-21.

Over five years, the Burford costs had risen by 20%. The speakers at two church houseparties challenged the church to proceed with the project, applying lessons from scripture. The first of these was at a comparatively early stage, before planning permission had been granted. 'We were in Acts 2,' explains Andrew Butcher, 'where verse 42 describes how the early church was devoted to God's word, to meeting together, to breaking bread and to prayer. The challenges were to make prayers "big, bold and scary", to reach out, and to work together. At the second houseparty we were looking at the book of Nehemiah, and how he exercised his reliance on God by praying and preparing well, and by expecting and tackling opposition.' Paring down on some costs was possible, but it was clear that the fundraising target had to be increased. By early 2016 they were 'within touching distance' of reaching the necessary funds. Rising costs are likely to reflect what is also happening at a domestic level, in the general cost of living. It takes 'big, bold and scary' faith to see such a project through to the end, for sure.

Chapter 7

Keeping everyone in touch

Any large project involves simultaneous action on several fronts, and careful co-ordination of each of the different areas of activity. While the elders or church council retain ultimate responsibility, much of the ongoing work is usually delegated to a building committee, a finance advisory group with deep experience in banking, finance and legal matters, and a Project Director. These people all shoulder a heavy load. In addition some churches hire the services, whether as a consultant or as short-term staff, of a professional fundraiser. It can be a great encouragement to these people to know that the church family is keeping in touch.

St Paul's & St George's used its website to build an online archive of photographs of the work in progress. It included a virtual walk-through of the new Welcome Area, then yet to be built. This area forms a significant feature of the renovated church, situated on a major bus route in the city centre.

On the wider communications front, local papers and news sites can keep the public informed of progress. Building projects costing millions of pounds raised from within the church family will naturally become a topic of conversation in a town or suburb.

Regular newsletters with occasional visits to the site to see progress—for the church family and for the local community—contribute hugely to keeping people in touch and, more, to retaining and building a sense of sympathy and of anticipation.

In St John the Evangelist, Carlisle, the church was not all of one mind when the idea for the building project was first announced. When a leaflet was distributed outlining the vision, and appealing for prayer and financial support, some members threatened to leave the church if the project went ahead. The PCC, naturally troubled at the way this threatened to undermine unity, resolved that each PCC member would take a share of the membership list, and arrange to visit people in their homes, to listen to their concerns in an unhurried way. This would prove to be a crucial means of showing that the leaders were listening. From that stage onwards informal conversations between leaders and the wider membership continued, alongside regular presentations in church services. Only one person decided to leave the church.

On the first Sunday that the new building was opened, with the underfloor heating switched on, several older ladies kicked their shoes off and actually danced with joy. They said they had waited fifty years to feel warm in church! Constant and varied communication was essential in winning almost everyone over to the vision.

The membership at Cornerstone, Nottingham was around 300 when the building project began, with an adult congregation of around 650, plus children. Radio Nottingham was keen to cover the story, and to show how its beginnings could be traced back to Peter Lewis's arrival in Nottingham some forty years earlier, to pastor a small Baptist church in Hyson Green.[23] While this level of overview reporting is perfect for the wider community, with its précis and snapshot approach, the church members themselves form a very different public.

To find the best means of communicating with the church family, and a chance to engage with people's questions, they settled on the following:

- **Newsletters**—to communicate progress. These became less frequent in later stages of the project as the building itself was a progress report.

23 Peter and his wife, Valerie, retired in February 2015 after 45 years of ministry among generations of townspeople and students.

- **Q&A meetings**—the leaders hosted regular meetings in the early stages to give a project update, followed by a forum to ask questions and then pray together. These drew 50-100 at a time, with attendance dropping off as people had their questions answered, and the building started to take shape.
- **Website**—where information was kept up-to-date and from which newsletters could be downloaded.
- **Webcam**—a webcam on site meant people could view progress as it was happening. A time lapse video of the demolition of the MFI warehouse which stood on the site was also produced.

Chapter 8

Difficult questions

Churches will sometimes have to address difficult, even painful questions which divide the congregation, but this is not always the case. Even for a church the size of St Paul's & St George's, Edinburgh it did not happen.

At Cornerstone there were two questions, both good questions, on which it took time to gain agreement. The first was about the benefit of building over renting. The church was growing now, without the constraint of managing premises. Could this not just continue? The second question concerned the relative benefits of dividing into smaller congregations, which could more easily have sought rented accommodation, and obviated the need or purchase. 'When it came to key votes on buying land and committing to the building contract, the proposals were carried with overwhelming majorities, and God preserved our unity through the time,' said Paul Couchman. 'Only a very small proportion of people chose to leave the church.'

For St Nicholas a matter which raised particular problems was the future of the Campaigners work.[24] The fact that the church council had on several occasions declared its commitment to preserve this work did not seem to allay fears. The difficulty arose from a need to sell the hall where the Campaigners met.

Surely God would lead in this, as he had in everything else. Yet there seemed no obvious answer. The division of views was unhelpful and was hindering Christian fellowship among some. Comments and questions came in writing, in telephone calls, and in conversations with the

24 A national evangelical movement with uniformed groups in many churches.

church staff and with church council members.

In a last effort to win the confidence of those who were disaffected, a final open meeting was planned for questions and answers. After this, the matter would be considered closed. It turned out to be a good meeting, with just over 20 people present, and everyone having the chance to speak and to feel they had been heard. While members of the building committee fielded the questions, their wives met to pray. At the end of the evening an envelope was handed in—a new financial pledge to replace one which had been rescinded earlier. The Holy Spirit was at work changing hearts, changing minds, changing attitudes.

No one doubted the vital and distinctive role played by Campaigners in the life of the church. A considerable amount of effort had already gone into scouring the town for a suitable alternative venue. A boys' school had been a possibility. It would have given enough space in halls and classrooms, but the Campaigner leaders felt, understandably, that being spread around the building would lose a sense of cohesion. Use of the school would also have incurred considerable expense. But this would have been offset by the loss of maintenance cost of the hall, which was eating into church funds.

A final decision on the sale of the hall was to be taken by the church council the following week. The outcome was awaited with more than a little interest.

On that morning, the Rector Miles Thomson and his wife, Sara, were reading in Proverbs 21, which opens with a strong affirmation of God's sovereignty: 'The King's heart is in the hands of the Lord; he directs it like a watercourse wherever he pleases.' Christians can sometimes lose that certainty of his ultimate control. Here was another reminder that everything was in his hands. It was unanimously agreed by the church council that the hall be sold. Such unanimity was a precious thing. The way ahead for Campaigners was still not clear, but the confident vote that evening reflected the council's reliance on a sovereign God.

Many churches in the country which have moved forward in a project like this probably have a similar story to tell of understandable concern in relation to one group or another. To hear how each of those situations was resolved would be faith-building. In St Nicholas the dénouement was entirely unexpected, and surely an answer to people's prayers. The minister of the United Reformed Church made an approach, asking if the Campaigners would like to meet in his building. This was close to the leaders' own home, and provided excellent hall space and a much better kitchen for use by those working for cookery badges. Yet again a solution had been found which was better than people could have hoped for or imagined.

Some members in St John the Baptist, Burford thought the project too large; some that the church should be concentrating on mission, not on their buildings. However, these tended to be under-currents rather than widely-voiced opinions. No-one left the church.

Given the boldness of the vision, it was no surprise that, initially, a number of the Burford PCC members were uncertain and urged caution. Gradually more confidence was gained as they saw answers to prayer along the way. The response to the first fundraising appeal exceeded hopes, and in the end, every significant decision was passed unanimously. This unanimity was always regarded as a blessing and confirmation from God.

Chapter 9

Setting and maintaining the tone

On the principle that the leaders should lead, members of the church council (or the elders and deacons) are often invited to make their pledges two weeks before the main Gift Day for the congregation, and the total pledged is announced on the Sunday in between. This can set a tone and demonstrate that the leadership is united in its commitment.

On the first Gift Day in St Nicholas, people placed their envelopes in the boxes as they arrived for the service. After they had been brought to the front of the church, and received with prayer, Miles Thomson preached. The passage was from Philippians 3, which contrasted any merit on this earth with 'the surpassing greatness of knowing Christ Jesus'. Miles simply expounded what Paul wrote.

The evening service followed a similar pattern, with Johnny Juckes (now Rector of Kirk Ella in Humberside) preaching on Isaiah 40. The chapter brought a powerful reminder that God can be trusted. Halfway through the service, Colin and Hazel Maunsell, on a brief home assignment, were interviewed about their work in Ethiopia. It was fitting to express commitment to them on this particular Sunday. The building project could not be allowed to preoccupy a mission-minded church or to divert resources from mission giving.

Sunday by Sunday, the teaching of Scripture addressed issues in people's minds. That summer Miles was preaching a series on the Songs of Ascent—the psalms sung by the people of Israel as they travelled to Jerusalem for special feasts. They were psalms of pilgrimage from which strong parallels could be drawn. In Israel then, as in Sevenoaks, a group of God's people were on a journey. By the end of July Miles had reached Psalm 133 with its clear plea for unity. Unity in the gospel was of far greater importance than anything else. Whatever people felt about the plans for the Undercroft, St Nick's must guard its unity.

Tony Wilmot was not only the driving force behind the Undercroft, but also Chairman of the St Nick's mission committee; he could not ignore the real and pressing needs of the global south. In August that year he preached with authority on Jesus' own words: 'The poor you will always have with you.' Here, he said, was an unusual opportunity to give sacrificially for God's glory. Again it was the teaching of Scripture being applied to the questions of the moment.[25]

If the Bible is our guide for all that we believe and all that we do, it has to remain in the forefront of our thinking. That is what it means to be an evangelical church. And the preaching on Sundays and daily Bible reading in homes play a very significant role in keeping projects on course, in proportion, and—all importantly—focused on their spiritual goal.

Maintaining unity will be a major aspect of maintaining 'the tone'. Lack of unity can so easily undermine leadership and have a poor effect on the way the church is perceived locally. It will take pastoral skill to maintain the tone, and keep the church together as a worshipping and witnessing community when there are differing comfort levels with building plans. While church leaders work diligently at maintaining unity, it would be naïve to think this is always possible to maintain it in our fallen world.

Those who feel the money should be going overseas could be invited to give to the mission fund rather than to the building project. But if in the end people resolve to leave and to worship elsewhere, then that decision, though sad, has to be respected. They should be assured of a

25 Helen Roseveare, renowned medical missionary in what is now the Democratic Republic of Congo, was also a driving force behind the building project in her church: St Elizabeth's, Dundonald, to the east of Belfast.

welcome back if at any stage they feel it right to return.

Life would certainly be far easier without any building project at all. Again and again it is Scripture's central thrust that keeps churches going: the thread traced from Genesis to Revelation of a missionary God with an ever-contemporary message for everyone to hear.

Chapter 10

Building for the gospel

Building for the Gospel, the title of this book, is, in a sense, what all church life is about. The Apostle Paul wrote to the Corinthian Christians about building for the gospel in their own lives:

> *By the grace God has given me, I laid a foundation as an expert builder, and someone else is building on it. But each one should be careful how he builds. For no one can lay any foundation other than the one already laid, which is Jesus Christ. If any man builds on this foundation using gold, silver, costly stones, wood, hay or straw, his work will be shown for what it is, because the Day will bring it to light. It will be revealed with fire, and the fire will test the quality of each man's work. If what he has built survives, he will receive his reward. If it is burned up, he will suffer loss; he himself will be saved, but only as one escaping through the flames.*
> (1 Corinthians 3: 10-15)

Leaders of church groups and activities are, all the time, 'building' in the lives of their members. God has given special gifts to some in the church so that—together and individually—the whole church family can be built up. In his letter to the Christians in Ephesus, Paul was clear about his aim: '...until we all reach unity in the faith and in the knowledge of the Son of God and become mature, attaining to the whole measure of the fulness of Christ' (Ephesians 4:12-13). This goal must be at the heart of any community of Christians.

Building for the gospel beyond our church

Building projects open up all sorts of possibilities for ancillary use of the premises, and the church family will bring dreams and ideas of ways they would like to see the new facility used: for specialist lectures, concerts, activities for local children... These put the church on the map for a wide-ranging public. That can only be good, so long as the administrative and cleaning loads do not become intolerable, and outside use does not crowd out the church's own needs.

In each of the churches featured, the church council invited a senior church member to consult first with leaders of present activities as to their hopes and aspirations for the new or re-ordered building; and then to open the same question to everyone in the church with regard to additional uses. Members of the church council, or of the church building committee, also talked with counterparts in churches that had already completed such a project. There is always much to share, and much to learn from those who are further ahead; and from accrued wisdom from professional experience.

Church life can sometimes be perceived by its members simply in terms of 'us and God'. The call to be salt and light in society, and to bring the good news of the gospel to friends, neighbours and colleagues, can slip off the edge of Christian thinking. The whole earth belongs to God, and Christians are in a sense reclaiming it for him. This applies in different ways to teachers, businessmen, medics and so forth, and everyone needs help in learning how to apply biblical principles in their work. A local church may not have specialists in all these areas, but leaders can point people in the right direction for stimulus and guidance.

Through praying, we can also build for the gospel in the lives of people we have never met. Our churches' missionaries are engaged in a wide range of activities across the continents: literature ministry, church planting, mission personnel work, student evangelism... Some serve in the UK offices of overseas missions. Whether on the front-line or in the back room they are all working to strengthen Christ's church around the world. And as church members get behind them in prayer, they are themselves building for the gospel across continents in villages and small towns, on university campuses and in the world's megacities.

Thinking Christianly

A casual observer would be forgiven for thinking Christianity out of place in the postmodern world: superseded, redundant. A more reflective person might wonder how the whole basis of modern western civilization could have been so quickly overturned.

In the mid 1980s John Stott coined the phrase 'double listening', saying Christians must listen to the word (the Bible) and listen to the world. Then we will be able to relate one to the other, and engage with the questions which people are asking. Preaching and teaching in our churches must help Christians to be double-listeners.

The idea of an objective body of truth has been completely eroded in our highly-individualistic and relativist culture. It might seem quaint to think of the Bible as our authority for what to believe and how to live; Jurassic Park may seem the best place for preachers.

Relating the Word to the world is a learned skill. Building for the gospel must include the task of building in people's lives to equip them as Christians in the here and now: as Christian parents, neighbours, and friends; and as Christians in the workplace. Let us never underestimate the wholly different mindset of the Christian. It takes time for people to absorb Christian values; a Christian worldview cannot be microwaved. We must work hard at helping one another to learn, love, and obey Scripture. Western society has moved a long way since the 1960s in attitudes to authority. For a generation, children have learned in school that their own interpretation of what they read is as valid as the author's intent, so it is not surprising that young Christians find it hard to grasp a sense of Scripture being not our 'guide' but our authority—our authority on what is true, and our authority on how to behave.

As we have already noted, this book is not about how the church can instil a sense of scripture's authority, but only about the premises needed, to provide a place for teaching and learning, for encouraging and imbibing; as well as for corporate and public worship.

Commuters in the congregation

Commuting is a feature of life in satellite towns and suburbs around all our major cities. The sheer numbers who pile off the trains every evening, and often don't get home until late, mean midweek church life has its limitations. Churches need to get behind people in the hard places of business and commerce and pray for them. Tired commuters have little enough time with their families and may find home groups or other evening meetings just too hard to get to. Different ways need to be found of helping them to 'dialogue' with the Bible for themselves, to interrogate it, to prove it as a trustworthy and sufficient guide, both for the big questions in their professions and for everyday living.

Even before the St Nicholas Undercroft was completed, it was agreed in principle that the next step would be to recruit an additional member to the church staff. This person would get alongside the many leaders (in the children's work, youth work, home groups, weekly meetings etc) to equip and resource them, provide whatever on-the-job training and support they needed, and keep a constant eye open for those with overload. He would also nurture a future generation of leaders. The job title was eventually agreed as Director of Pastoring and Training. It was essentially an enabling job, a bit like that of a team coach. Someone nicknamed it 'church bodybuilder'.

Philip de Grey-Warter (now Rector of Fowey) joined the staff in this role. While appropriate buildings are needed for effective ministry, having the right people in the right jobs to enable that ministry is just as vital. With Philip on board, two major new initiatives became possible.

First he and the other clergy were able to look out for emerging leaders in whom time and training should be invested. Phil and his wife, Naomi, ran a training course for groups of six or eight people at a time, culminating in a residential weekend. Over the course of a program like this, the members get to know one another, and there is a team spirit of learning together. 'The aim,' said Philip, 'was to enthuse and envision members for biblical ministry and spiritual leadership, and begin to equip them for it.'

There was no pressure on anyone to take up a leadership role straight away, nor any pressure on Phil to put someone in a gap which needed to be plugged. It is vital to have people in the right roles, whether working with children, teenagers, home groups or in any other capacity.

Secondly there was *Toolbox*. This is now used in different forms around the country. On an occasional basis, evening services are replaced by seminars on a range of subjects. These seminars look at the practical aspects of what it means to be a Christian in the world of business, commerce, and education; in the family; in the community. It would be misleading to say there is no evening worship on those Sundays, for the whole evening is an act of worship, as church members seek to work out how the Lordship of Christ affects their lives.

Good, flexible, modern premises give openings for many different ways of engaging the minds and hearts of Christians and of those who have not professed faith. Toolbox, lunchtime meetings for those working locally, pre-school groups, 'Just Daddy and Me', retired men's lunches, women's evangelism, apologetics seminars, student Bible studies—our aim is surely to nurture the life of Christ in people, the life of the One through whom everything was created, and in whom all things hold together (Colossians 1:17). In a world of fragmented and disintegrated thinking—disconnected from the present and disconnected from the past—to be reminded of things 'holding together' in Christ is profound.

Our grasp of the gospel and of its bearing on life and society always needs to be stretched. We need to learn how to apply its timeless truth to contemporary needs, and to engage the minds and hearts of a new generation. Our work of building for the gospel will not be completed until the Lord Jesus returns.

Paul's letters to the New Testament churches reflect a perceptive grasp of human weakness and of spiritual aspiration. The famous Victorian preacher, Charles Haddon Spurgeon, coined the phrase 'bibline blood'. He wanted his own church family at the Metropolitan Tabernacle in London's Elephant and Castle to get the Bible into their bloodstreams, so to speak. That is the spirit of Paul's writing where biblical values become the 'pulse' of day-to-day living. The 'one anothers' (Appendix 1) express these values as they touch on the way Christians relate to each other. We will always have to keep on working at these things.

Chapter 11

A lot of money!

Faith and finance are intertwined in a story like this. Media pundits may tell us how successful an able orator can be in exhorting people to give. But building projects need serious-minded and long-term giving, and oratory cannot produce that. Building projects will stretch a church. They will prove our faith, and they will strengthen faith.

Only the Holy Spirit can convince people of the need for a project to move forward. The whole church membership, or at least the majority of members, have to want it to happen or it will not gain the necessary financial backing. The stories of all the building projects featured here tell of real joy in giving.

Giving is a personal matter, serious, and for church members to resolve before God with their families or on their own. People should not feel pressured to give. Many churches adopt the principle that the pastor is not informed how much anyone gives. That knowledge is confidential to the building committee treasurer, and whoever is assisting them. In whatever way people respond to the building project—whether enthusiastically, sympathetically, neutrally or antagonistically—the pastor has a responsibility under God to be their pastor, and nothing should be allowed to affect that, or be perceived to affect it.

Typically a church will have few if any high earners; more will be in the middle-income group. And then there are pensioners, young singles, and newly-married couples, many with more limited incomes; others will be working voluntarily or be unemployed.

We can imagine some of the thoughts going through people's minds. How might things be juggled? To see a project through, everyone needs to pull together; to give what they can, indeed to give all they can. The church is a family, and there is no distinction in that regard between those in well-paid professions and those in more modestly-paid jobs. Some can give large sums of money; others less. Equally, some are time-rich; others time-poor. In addition to all this, the building fund can't be allowed to take over church life, or overshadow the need for other church giving.

The Dewsbury story was very unusual, lasting barely eight months after the building was identified. The whole project cost £500,000, considerably less than others, but a very large sum for a church of its kind in the north of England. This included an interest-free loan of £50,000 from a Christian trust, repayable over ten years. Other giving was not affected.

Paul Couchman of Cornerstone, Nottingham said people often enquire what spurred the church's giving.

'It is one of the more amazing aspects of our story. It is the question I am asked most about, and actually has the simplest answer: A clearly articulated vision, strongly held by the whole church. We focused this around Psalm 78:4

We will not hide [God's works] from their descendants;
we will tell the next generation
the praiseworthy deeds of the Lord,
his power, and the wonders he has done.

We wanted this investment to last well beyond our own lives. Our vision was for a hundred years of gospel witness in our city and beyond, if the Lord didn't return sooner.' He added, 'The church responded right from the outset. In fact, we had raised well over £1million before we had even found land! We saw our building project just as one little milestone in one small corner of God's great gospel story. We were a part of something so much bigger.

Peter Lewis preached through Nehemiah as the Cornerstone project got underway.[26] *We were encouraged by the stories of other churches*

26 Sermons available at cornerstonechurch.org.uk

The mountain-climbing analogy

Building projects can be likened to climbing a steep mountain, as Paul Batchelor explained to members of the Round Church in Cambridge (now at St Andrew the Great, better known as StAG). In both, he said, we have a clear objective in view and an unshakeable guide.

- We know the route to take, and we have the best possible back-up team.
- There are obstacles to navigate from the earliest stages, and at times the going can be very tough. We know we can trust our guide, but we still at times experience doubt and fear. Sometimes we feel like giving up and turning back.
- As we look back we snatch a glimpse of the view. We can see some progress has been made. The end seems more worthwhile, and the seemingly 'impossible' becomes the 'very difficult'.
- We must keep the summit in our mind's eye, even when clouds descend. People have made financial sacrifices, and are honouring their promises. We remember this, and we think of the spiritual benefits that reaching the summit—gaining the new facilities—will offer. It spurs us on.
- The summit seems closer, then recedes. We suddenly meet a new difficulty, another long haul, which we had not anticipated.
- We have to accept that not everyone in the group will make equal progress. Doubt can keep creeping back, and for some this will be a genuine impediment. How vital for the leaders to trust the guide implicitly, and to take others with them in that.
- Every so often, pause for rest and refreshment, take a look

at the view and remind yourself of progress made. But don't loiter too long.

- For success in climbing a difficult mountain, we need to dig deep into resources of stamina and energy. To keep our eyes on the summit will take all our spiritual reserves.
- Once the summit is reached, we can see other summits to aim for, which were previously not in view.

that had trodden the same path that we were just setting out on. We gave everyone a copy of Building for the Gospel to read too. As we progressed from one stage to the next, it was so helpful for other churches to share their experiences with us.

We were clear that funding for overseas mission should not suffer while we were doing this project. We emphasized that giving for the building should be over and above normal giving, as a 'once in a generation' opportunity that God had entrusted to us. We are grateful to God that we maintained support for all of our overseas workers and were even able to send new workers overseas during that time. It's hard to say whether giving to the regular ministry of the church was affected as we were doing all of this during a period of recession within the UK and we had some of the same financial challenges as may other churches did at the time.'

In Edinburgh, St Paul's & St George's spent five consecutive Sundays looking at New Testament teaching about money, and Jesus' attitude towards money. Only one of those weeks was on giving; the others covered biblical principles of stewardship in general. This was a year before the first pledge day. In this way church members had plenty of time to process and put into practice the biblical principles which they had learned.

As the first pledge day drew nearer, Dave Richards preached a series of sermons on the life of Moses leading the Israelites out of Egypt. This brought good lessons in trusting God for the future, for the unknown.

Giving early makes a difference

Where people come on board early with gifts, there is distinct benefit. Understandably some hold back. They are not confident that sufficient money will be raised. More than that, substantial seed money would be needed for the feasibility study alone. From here it may be concluded that the 'do-nothing' option is the best way forward. And who wants to sink money into a feasibility study which will have no marked benefit in the short term, to relieve the pressures here and now. It can take time for this kind of skeptic mindset to change. Time, prayer, and the work of the Holy Spirit.

Once people see the level of giving rise, they too will give. In a major project like this, the balance between those who will give in faith and those who want first to see success round the corner is critical. 'Lord, I believe. Help my unbelief,' must surely be many people's prayer as they make their gifts and fill in their pledges before it becomes definite that permission has been granted for the project to go ahead. And they probably become the major prayer force in asking for others to be moved from skepticism to risk-taking faith.

It is a false hope to think that presently-unknown trusts 'out there' will somehow save a congregation from having to give money for building projects. If we think of ourselves as stewards of the church's ministry in our town or city, in our time, the reason for our giving, and our encouraging one another to give, becomes clearer.

Three or four weeks before the formal launch of the St Ebbe's, Oxford building project, Trevor Rayment, the church treasurer, wrote individually to members of the church leadership:

I am writing to members of the church council, the Premises Development Group, and the senior staff team, to ask us to be amongst the first to commit financial support to the Building for Growth project and to ask if you would be prepared to make your pledge a week in advance of the main launch.

I would like to share with you a few thoughts to help us all as we choose how to support this project. The first thought is why ask that we should pledge first? A number of reasons might be proposed. The most common reason is to provide an example or evidence of commitment to others who might be asked to give later: St Ebbe's church members and external trust funds. This is the advice given in successful but secular fund raising.

I am not convinced by this advice since it brings moral pressure and it risks being seen that the 'leaders did well'. This is not the giving that our Lord commends. The better reason is that which we see in the Gospel accounts. When the crowds were fed, Jesus simply asked the disciples what they had. They gave it to him and he did miraculous things. They did what they were asked in a circumstance of overwhelming need.

As those who have become convinced that this project is the way forward for building the gospel at St Ebbe's, I think that it is right to put what each of us has in the hands of the Lord.

I believe that each of us is called to answer the question 'what do we have to give?' Let us put what we have in the Lord's hands and see what he can do. The work is his to do. Therefore I would encourage you not to think of the (scary) sums of money that might be needed for the various scenarios which have been presented. That is the Lord's choice not ours.

Simply ask 'what can I give?'

Please pray for wisdom for your own decisions and pray for equal wisdom for all of us in a leadership position.

Whatever happens, this is for the glory of God and the growth of the gospel.

With best wishes
Trevor

Our motives are of real importance. We need to take stock before God, and it's important to give good notice of pledge dates, so people can con-

Effective giving

There are both practical and spiritual lessons to learn from a project like this:

- All gifts are important and valuable. No gift is too small to consider. All promote a sense of involvement and commitment.
- Sustained, sacrificial giving is the most effective. Regular giving becomes part of one's way of life. The sums donated earn interest, and often attract tax relief. The combined effect is very striking. In the St Nick's project, the combined income from interest and tax recoveries was over £500,000.
- The most tax-effective way is giving through the Gift Aid scheme (for lump sums) or through giving agencies like Stewardship or the Charities Aid Foundation (CAF).
- For individuals and families, it is important to plan and budget for giving. It may help to set the sum aside in a separate account. In that way it does not get diverted unintentionally.
- If you cannot afford to give much money, give your abilities, and don't underestimate the value of giving time to prayer.
- Be a cheerful giver (2 Corinthians 9:7).
- Remember that all we have comes from God. We are merely giving back a small part of that (1 Chronicles 29:14).
- God rewards our giving many times over, spiritually.

sider carefully how they should respond. This follows the Apostle Paul's practice and model (see 2 Corinthians 8 and 9) when he arranged a collection for the poor saints. It is instructive to read these well-known Giving chapters from the perspective of the arrangements the Apostle set in place.[27]

27 For this less-often-talked-about angle on financial giving, see 'The Gift of Accountability' by Chris Wright in *The Grace of Giving* (listed on p111).

Reasons for giving

There is a popular cartoon with a minister giving announcements in a Sunday service. It runs like this:

> **Minister:** *The good news is that we already have all the money we need for our building work.*

(The cartoonist shows the faces of the congregation. Everyone looks pleased, relieved, assured. Someone else has spared them from having to give. That is good news! But things change in the next frame…)

> **Minister:** *But the bad news is that it is still in your bank accounts.*

We laugh because it is funny. That kind of caricature has a wonderful simplistic charm. But such an approach will never draw the hard cash it is looking for. There is a world of difference between what are sometimes called the 'ethics of guilt' and the 'ethics of gratitude'. If several, even many, people are embarrassed into writing a cheque for two or three hundred pounds, it might mend a leaking roof or replace rotting boards. That is the ethics of guilt in action. Consciences are appeased, and there is a sense of having done one's bit. But the ethics of guilt will never be imaginative and creative. Nor will they edify the giver.

The ethics of guilt will not, cannot, create the fitting new premises for corporate worship and for evangelism which churches up and down the country need today. Very different are the ethics of gratitude, where giving springs from thankfulness to God, truly believing that all we have comes from him, and being thankful that we ourselves have been bought with a price by Jesus' death on a cross. That makes all the difference in the world. How can we give him enough in return? And how can we not give with joy?

The following diagrams show the breakdown of income from Cornerstone, Nottingham and from Cuckfield. Others would be similar, in demonstrating the joint effort of those with large incomes, those with middle incomes and those with smaller incomes, of pensioners, students, and young people with pocket money. These are spiritual enterprises, not a competition for the size of gift. People must be invited to give joyfully, and as they are able.

Paul Couchman from Cornerstone explains: 'almost all the giving came from church members. One-off giving from gift days was very important initially to encourage further giving, but it was the regular standing orders which were most important to our long-term planning, and we are relying on these to pay off the mortgage.'

Cornerstone: Breakdown of giving (graphs 1-3)

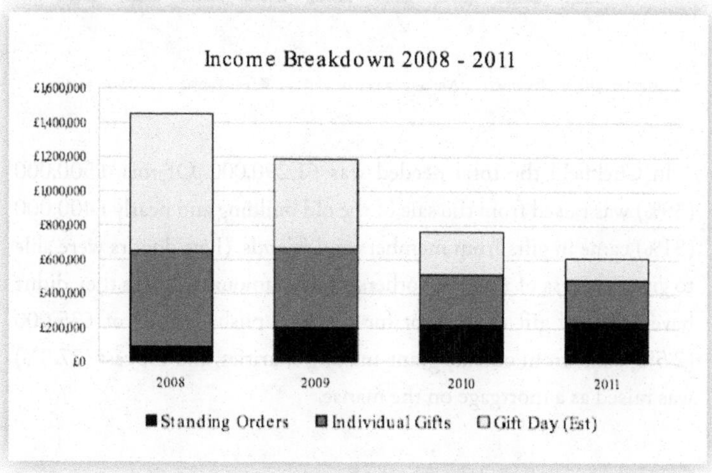

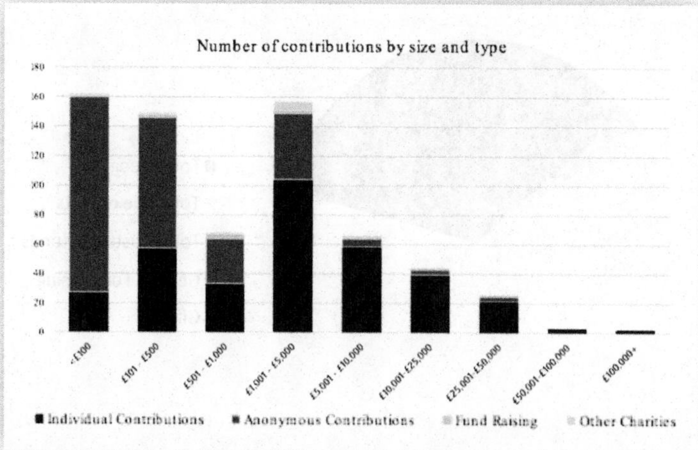

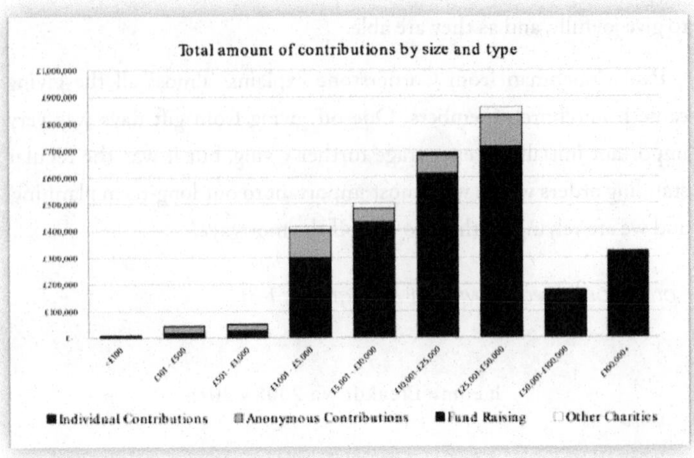

In Cuckfield the total needed was £1,290,000. Of this, £500,000 (39%) was raised from the sale of the old building and nearly £400,000 (31%) came in gifts from members and friends. (Five donors were able to give in excess of £25,000; others smaller amounts.) Here they didn't have a special gift day except for the final push. A total of £35,000 (2.5%) came from outside grant-making charities, and the rest (27.5%) was raised as a mortgage on the manse.

Cuckfield: Split of total fundraising by source:

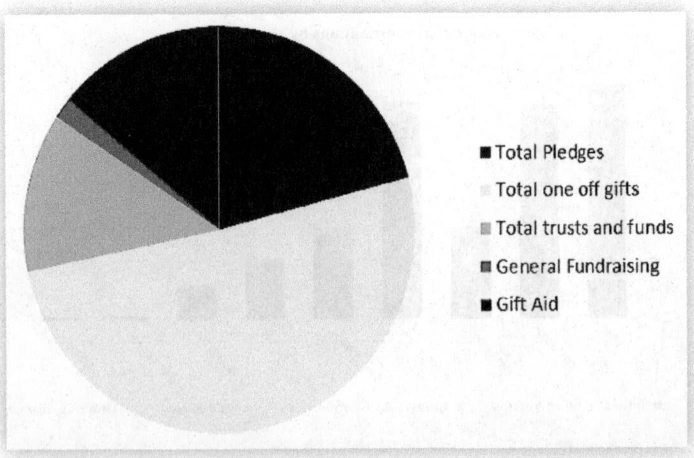

Jesus is very interested in giving

Jesus is very interested in giving, and in Mark's Gospel we read that he sat himself down right opposite the place in the temple where the offerings were left, and watched the crowd putting their money into the temple treasury.

> *Many rich people threw in large amounts. But a poor widow came and threw in two very small copper coins, worth only a fraction of a penny. Calling his disciples to him, Jesus said, 'I tell you the truth, this poor widow has put into the treasury more than all the others. They all gave out of their wealth; but she, out of her poverty, put in everything—all she had to live on.* (*Mark 12:41-44*)

Some of the most faithful giving in the course of these projects will be from those of limited means who give what they can afford, in cash in envelopes, weekly or monthly, over several years. Motivation is everything in God's sight. These people give out of their love for him. An envelope was dropped through the door of one rectory from a woman whose husband was ill and out of work, promising £10 per month in cash for the building fund. To receive notes like that is very humbling. They mean more than the writers know. However creating new buildings will also require a lot of people to give substantial sums 'out of their wealth'. How vitally important it is, in a spiritual sense, that these greatly-needed major donors should be giving for the right reasons too.

Passing the million milestone

After an initial appeal, pledges often creep up only slowly, and at times seem to be stuck. Once a certain milestone has been reached (£1m in the case of St Nicholas) the inflow of pledges often stalls. This period can bring feelings of uncertainty and at times, for some, near despair. When that stage was reached at St Nicholas, just over 300 of the 520 members had given. It was a classic point for this to happen; the initial excitement was beginning to wane but it was too early for any visible signs of progress. Detailed designs were still being developed, and would possibly push the initial estimates further up. But the gifts already received and the tax recovered on them did represent a significant financial milestone.

The Milestone brochure arrived in every member's home when some were already beginning to feel the effects of giving-fatigue; others who had been hesitant earlier were even more hesitant now—interest rates had fallen and those with substantial savings had taken an economic beating.

The brochure was written jointly by David Brewster, Legal Director for the Investment Management Regulatory Organization (IMRO), who chaired the Finance Advisory Group, and Paul Batchelor, building project Treasurer. It laid out the matter clearly:

> *God has faithfully met our prayers. He has removed all other obstacles from our path. Now he is challenging us to make some sacrifices, and to return to him part of the gifts he has given to us. We should welcome the challenge.*
>
> *The time has come to put doubts and division behind us, and to unite in the cause of the One whom we all desire to serve, and whose gospel we wish to proclaim more effectively here in Sevenoaks. It is not a matter for others, but for each and every one of us.*
>
> - *Of those who have already given generously, we ask, can you do more?*
> - *Of those who have made a start, we ask, can you go further?*
> - *Of those who have waited, we ask, is not now the time to start?*
> - *Of those who have doubted, we ask, can you now see these signs of God's will and join us?*
>
> *It has perhaps fallen to us to have the privilege to equip St Nicholas for many generations to come. Two years ago we were moved to pledge almost a million pounds for this cause. Most of this is now being faithfully contributed. Please pray that, in a few weeks' time, we will be similarly moved so that, together, with God's help, we can do the same again.*

The leaflet closed with the increasingly familiar words of the Apostle Paul to the Christians in Ephesus: 'Now to him who is able to do immeasurably more than all we ask or imagine, according to his power that is at work within us, to him be glory in the church and in Christ Jesus throughout all generations, for ever and ever!'

Eating elephants

The celebrated Q&A in the Time Manager system runs:

> Q: *'How do you eat an elephant?'*
>
> A: *'Bit by bit.'*

Is that a facile question for executives who conduct their lives around its eight-point diary system? It would seem not. Elephant-sized tasks in any field need to be broken down. It is no different in churches. We must all break down our elephantine tasks and, with God's help, tackle them bit by bit with the human-sized energy he has given us. Hudson Taylor moved from 'Impossible' through 'Difficult' to 'Done' in just this way. He walked up and down Brighton beach on 25 June 1865, praying for '24 skilful, willing workers' to go to China. What faith to ask for two dozen people, who as yet had no Chinese language, to make an impact on a massive country with an ancient culture steeped in 'isms' and folk religion! It sounded impossible. But this was the first step in taking the gospel of Christ to its seemingly impenetrable inland provinces. China was the size of a whole herd of Time Manager's notional elephants, not just one. But two missionaries for each province and two for Mongolia was a start. Similarly, the cost of a building project can seem impossible, but when looked at bit by bit, the figures can come into focus.

The adventure of fundraising

Where gospel purposes are in view, many churches will not want to apply for funds from the national lottery. Extra giving is seen as a privilege for church members, a chance for them to express their love of Christ in a tangible way. In Leyland all church members received a personal visit from the church warden and his wife, on behalf of the Vision Builders team, specifically to invite a pledge. In Edinburgh and in Sevenoaks the congregations were invited in small groups to hear about the plans over coffee and cake, and to receive a special Giving Pack; this enabled all church members to talk about the project and to think and pray seriously not only about how much to give, but about how and when to give to greatest effect.

As with many churches, the St Nick's congregation included several wives whose husbands do not share their faith and commitment. It was not felt right for those wives to put pressure on the family budget for a project like this. Two moving stories of people in this situation were to emerge. One such wife received an unexpected legacy, from which she felt able to give without affecting the family budget. Another found herself with a tax repayment she was not anticipating. Again, this was money out of which she could give. These were gifts from the heart. Coming as they did from wives who wanted to observe the biblical pattern of not antagonizing an unconverted husband, they were especially meaningful. It was as if God had provided the means.

ẍ

'There was an expectation (or hope) from some,' said Paul Couchman, 'that external funding would help raise the money needed for Cornerstone. We explored this, but found it very time-consuming and it resulted in only one donation. Our vision was for a home for gospel ministry and mission and there aren't many organizations prepared to sponsor that.

'We had a strong conviction that the project was a challenge of faith that God had given to us as a church; and that it would have felt disingenuous to ask others for funding. External sources can be attractive, especially if a church is to provide community facilities as part of their gospel ministry. But other sources could also bring constraint if funding comes with strings attached.'

For Cornerstone, only £60,000 (1%) came from external donations, over half of this from other churches in the city. No church reported a substantial proportion of income from an external source, other, that is, than the Chancellor of the Exchequer, through Gift Aid.

Some churches have written to former members, to invite them to contribute to the building fund, which many may like to do, especially if they were part of the church family for some years, or at a formative point in their lives.

Where a church owns property for staff use, a question has been raised by at least one church council as to whether the house needs to belong to the church. If, for example, one or more church members could purchase the property, and make it available to the church at a peppercorn rent for an agreed number of years, this could free up a considerable sum for a building fund in the short or medium term.

Church members' fundraising ideas

Fundraising initiatives can be fun and build community along the way.

One church opened a talent fund with a gift of £200. Anyone could ask for money from the fund to invest in personal money-making projects. It could cover, for example, ingredients for baking, or material for sewing. The children could receive money for ingredients to make cakes to sell to the church family.

Here are a few examples of what people have done:

- Cleared attics and sold what they don't need on eBay, or in a local auction sale; These have included signed cricket bats, autographed first editions of books etc;
- Offered New Testament Greek lessons, or introductory courses in a modern language; or DIY lessons;
- Made baby clothes or cushion covers to order;
- Painted watercolours of the church and sold prints; or accepted commissions to paint watercolours of houses or local scenes;
- Gathered recipes for a church cookbook, always enhanced by

contributions from children and teenagers;

- Put on a special concert by the choir;
- Used a spare bedroom (or a student-child's bedroom in term-time) for language-school students, or to host airbnb guests;
- Held a promise auction.[28]

Everyone can get involved. The youth group, or students in their vacation, can be employed as casual gardeners, car-washers, and decorators, and give a proportion of their earnings to the building fund. Children can make cards and bookmarks to sell. One church gave all the younger children a tube of Smarties. There was a deal attached—when empty it became a piggy bank for the building project. They too could become a part of the giving team, a discipline and an honour they would always remember.

While adding to the income streams, fundraising activities also strengthen the church's sense of community. St Paul's & St George's, with a congregation drawing in many students and young professionals, used sports sponsorship in a creative way. One group abseiled off the Forth Road Bridge, sponsored by the metre. Others ran the Edinburgh Marathon, either as individuals or as part of a relay team. These runners would train by running together in the evenings, and draw in friends outside church to train with them. In a big church like St Paul's and St George's some had not met each other before; here was another means of growing and strengthening friendships, within and outside the church family.

Having fun along the way does not detract from the seriousness of giving. Direct giving will always be the major source of income.

28 An auction of skills or assets. For example a church member could invite bids for providing a certain number of evenings of baby-sitting; or for lending DIY skills to erect a fence, or put up shelving. If members own holiday homes, they could invite bids for a week's stay in the home. These are typically light-hearted church family events. One building project manager wrote of their auction as 'particularly memorable', as his house group successfully bid for a year's supply of cake for the group!

- **'Buy at'** In common with a growing number of charities and churches, St Paul's and St George's joined the 'Buy at' scheme. Through this they were able to engage the help of Tesco, Amazon, and John Lewis, together with a range of other major UK names. These companies give a percentage of income to a named charity for all online purchases. A link to 'Buy at' was put on the church website. As church members got into the habit of ordering online and naming St Paul's and St George's as their chosen charity, an income stream was created which would continue to benefit the church.
- **Clearing the building** There has been a market for pews to be used in pubs for several years; and church members with larger rooms may like to purchase a short pew, or a length of one, to have in their home. But what else could raise money when a church building is cleared? Ebay has no limits. Cast iron radiators could raise a few hundred pounds. We can no longer assume anything is worthless just because we ourselves no longer have use for it.

God keeps his promises

Even with a seven-figure sum in the bank, there can be hurdles ahead, especially when a church is dependent on permissions from others outside the situation. This is always the case for Anglican churches, as we have seen, where the Diocesan Chancellor holds the authority to grant permission in his gift. They may feel they cannot responsibly rely on the rest of the money coming in. This was the situation in Sevenoaks up to just a few days before the time when the tenders would run out. News of the Chancellor's reluctance to grant permission came on Monday; the tenders would become void by noon on Friday that week.

A revised business plan was hastily prepared. It demonstrated the faithful record of giving over the previous two years; explained how the cash flow would work during construction; and set out the consequences of delays in going ahead. It also chronicled the depth of financial and business experience which members of the Finance Advisory Group brought with them.

But the Chancellor still had questions. With the prospect of costs escalating, or even of having to re-tender, the pressure was on. A further letter was written that Wednesday evening, answering all the questions raised—about the profile of giving, and the number of people who had given to the project. It also sought to allay fears that some might have been coerced into pledging more than they could afford. Janet Batchelor delivered it personally to the Chancellor's home on the Thursday morning.

At 10.00am on Friday, Miles Thomson received a call. The Diocesan Chancellor had agreed to grant the Faculty. There were only two hours left to spare. God had taken the church family right down to the wire.

That Sunday evening towards the end of the service there was an enormous clap of thunder and simultaneous lightning. As the service closed the arch of a bright rainbow served as a reminder that God keeps his promises.

QUICK CHECKLIST FOR US AS GIVERS

If you are involved with a church which embarks on a major building project you will want to consider prayerfully what part you may be called upon to play in contributing to the cost. Here are some of the questions you might wish to consider:

Is it financially appropriate for me to support this project?

Should I, and can I, increase my current giving or do I need to re-order my present priorities?

How much should I contribute and over what period?

Am I in a position to make one or more lump-sum gifts or should I plan to give a more modest sum more regularly?

Am I going to be giving out of income or capital?

What is my tax position, and how can I give most tax-effectively?

To give or not to give for this project?

Your decision on whether or not to support a particular project financially is a personal one. We each have personal—and often family—commitments that we need to honour. We also have preferences for the sort of causes we prefer to support; some like to support 'bricks and mortar' projects, others prefer to support people and activities. We need to pray and examine ourselves to ensure that we are making these decisions for the right reasons not out of selfishness or prejudice. Importantly we need to consider whether we are giving enough and for the right reasons. Having reached a conclusion through reflection and prayer we can commit to making our gifts cheerfully.

More giving or re-directed giving?

A major project often calls for sacrificial giving over a prolonged period. Many will be able to increase their giving; others may need to re-order their priorities. The choice is again a matter for personal reflection and prayer. Many people use the idea of 'tithing' as a measure of what it is appropriate to give. The idea of the tithe (giving a tenth of one's income) is a useful starting point but it can be too formulaic and is not always easy to interpret. For example, are we talking of gross income or income net of tax? Are there other exclusions? Should we take account of the stage of life we have reached? Ultimately, the choice and the measure are personal and made privately before God.

How much and over what period?

Ideas as to generosity, and what constitutes sacrificial giving, vary very widely. Many people welcome some means of calibrating what their contribution to a project might realistically be. For example the church might break down the total needed into smaller amounts. See the bar chart from Cornerstone, Nottingham in a previous chapter, for their actual figures.

Whatever the breakdown looked like for your church, the figures could be shown in a pyramid table showing numbers of people in a series of bands giving specific amounts over a specified period. People seem often to have a sense of what their contribution ought to be.

Early giving is especially helpful. It encourages others. Early gifts of significant lump sums are especially welcome; those with the means should do this. For many others, however, a substantial pledge has to be fulfilled gradually by regular more-modest gifts from income. Entering into a regular commitment of this kind often helps with personal or family budgeting.

Giving out of capital or income?

For many people the only realistic option is to give out of income.

However, some may have accumulated significant savings. Others may enjoy the benefit of a legacy or receive a substantial bonus and have the opportunity to give part or all of it away. Some people in or approaching retirement may choose to cash in part of their pension-pot to receive a cash lump sum. If the circumstances allow, these may provide the means for giving a lump-sum gift that will accelerate the flow of funds to the project. The most appropriate choice between these different options depends very much on one's personal circumstances; if in any doubt as to the best course of action, it is sensible to seek financial advice.

Am I giving tax-effectively?

Tax recoveries often constitute the largest single contribution to the financing of a major project so individual action to give as tax-effectively as possible is very important. The basis for this is the government's charitable 'gift aid' provision. The processes are simple and any UK-resident tax-payer should take advantage of them; gift aid increases the value of gifts from UK tax payers by 25%.

Chapter 12

Vacating the building

Each church will have stories to tell of the months they spend out of their building, while the work is in progress: stories of the new dynamic that this time gave, and then stories of their return.

The Cornerstone congregation had thought they would need to vacate the school by January 2010, but the school's building project was delayed for a range of reasons, so Cornerstone was able to relocate to the school's second site for a few months while work on their own new building was underway.

Rather than to vacate, the solution in St John the Baptist, Burford, was to work around the disruption in the church building itself. The Sunday School met in one end of the church while the main service was being held at the other end. Despite a certain flow of noise from one end to the other, the arrangement worked remarkably well for over 18 months. Temporary storage and other logistical matters had to be handled as best possible.

We pick up now on what happened at St Nicholas, Sevenoaks.

Leaving the church building

Just ten days after the Chancellor's permission had been received for the Undercroft to go ahead, the church family of St Nicholas moved out.

Major refurbishment can entail a long period out of the building. The final Sunday in the church building is bound to be a significant day for everyone. Some of the very elderly must wonder if they would worship there again. Enthusiasm for the plans from this sector of the church family in particular means a great deal. They are likely to find it harder than others to worship in a hired hall.

As St Nick's moved out, Miles Thomson preached from 1 Samuel 7:

'The Philistine army had been routed, and Samuel wanted to mark a great victory. He did so by setting up a large stone, which was like a war memorial, but with one big difference. It didn't contain the names of the dead—those who had died in battle—but just one name, the name of the living, the living God who had helped them to win the victory. As we think of building for the gospel we can say, as Samuel did, "In everything has the Lord helped us".

'That Stone was a powerful reminder. As they looked at it, it would strengthen their trust in the Lord for the next challenge. We can look back and rejoice. We can look ahead and trust because in everything has the Lord helped us too.' Quoting from Joseph Hart's hymn, Miles finished: 'So we'll praise him for all that is past, and trust him for all that's to come.'

A crèche was arranged for the evening service, so whole families could come if they wanted to. This was an historic day: the culmination of dreams and prayers over 30 years. The final hymn sung in the church before leaving took up from where Miles had finished in the morning. Everyone stood to sing:

How good is the God we adore,
Our faithful, unchangeable friend
Whose love is as great as his power,
And knows neither measure nor end.

The remaining lines were to wait for another fifteen minutes. First people all picked up a kneeler to carry it to the back of the church with them. This was a small help for the volunteer force who were to clear the building the next day, but also—and more importantly—a symbolic act. The whole church family was 'hands-on' in that earliest step of transforming the old St Nick's into what they had dreamed of, prayed for, and given for. Then everyone snaked up Six Bells Lane and on down to the church hall, where the singing of the hymn continued:

For Christ is the first and the last;
His Spirit will guide us safe home:
We'll praise him for all that is past
And trust him for all that's to come.

After committing to God in prayer all that lay ahead in this great adventure of faith, a large cake was cut and handed round. It had become a St Nick's tradition for all important occasions to be marked in this way.

Life outside the building

From now on, the weekly notice sheet would carry a large number on the top right hand side, with a countdown of the number of weeks to the return. The following Sunday it read 78.

Aware that on any given Sunday there might be visitors to a town parish church, Ian Dobbie, the Project Director, arranged a rota of volunteers to stand outside the church and point them in the right direction for the service. One such visitor was a charming Japanese lady. She was visiting London for the first time, and made the journey down to Sevenoaks one Sunday morning, especially to see the church. It wasn't its ancient foundation which had drawn her, nor had she heard about Building for the Gospel. But in the 1920s, a missionary called Elsie Baker had been sent out by St Nicholas to work in Osaka. Sometime during her 40 years in East Asia, she had planted the seed of the gospel in this Japanese visitor's life, others had since watered and God had given the growth. This lady's visit was a wonderful reminder of the way the local church is linked with the worldwide church, and of how one woman from a comfortable English parish can have an influence for Christ which will stand the test of time. Shinto-Buddhism, so much a part of Japanese culture, can seem virtually impenetrable.

At last the countdown finished, with its inevitable delays along the way, and almost two years later, the last evening service in the church hall closed with the first verse of the same hymn: 'How good is the God we adore!' The church family had been through two momentous years, and learned more of God's goodness in that time. The reverse process took place, along Six Bells Lane and to the west door of the church. Miles hesitated as he was about to announce the start of the second verse. Were 'the Dorothys' there yet? Dorothy Badman and Dorothy Corke walked a little more slowly than others, and everyone needed to be together for this. The two Dorothys were typical of a large band of elderly people who had been in St Nick's for decades. Faced with change, they did not react against it, but weighed the arguments. Not only were they accepting of it, but they welcomed it.

Chapter 13

Planning to move back

To entrust decisions to a small group who have a good aesthetic sense works well. The architects will provide a steer and the group can work with that, and within a budget, to decide on the final choices. It can be worth visiting several churches and perhaps the Christian Resources Exhibition to research possibilities. For the chairs the St Nicholas ambience team chose a pale terracotta fabric which catches the sun and adds a lightness to the church in a timeless and pleasing way. The carpet is an unobtrusive pale brown. Interior décor is conspicuous when it is not appropriate, and a joy to the eye when it is just right.

The people to help

The opening verses of Acts 6 lay out a dilemma and how it was resolved. The church needed extra help in the form of volunteers who could take responsibility for the distribution of food. What kind of people would they look for to fulfil this role? Those who were 'full of the Spirit and wisdom' (Acts 6:3).

So much of a church's life is dependent on volunteer staff who handle catering arrangements. As new premises create a range of new uses, the catering becomes a critical part of the church's life. Consistency and a gentle spirit are tested in the church kitchen. For a catering team to be led by someone who has a servant heart, is an encourager by nature, and can see the funny side to everything, is a wonderful tone-setter in any church. Marilynn Sowerby was just like that. For years she led a team of volunteers in St Nick's, always spotting the chance to draw in newcomers, enabling them to get to know others as they prepared food or washed up.[29] Helpers in the church kitchen and helpers in all the midweek activities, as Acts 6 shows, are playing a role which complements that of the pastor and the leadership team. While their time is spent in practical work, it will be done out of love for Christ, and with a desire to serve him.

A growing number of evangelical churches now participate in the interdenominational '9:38 Ministry Training Scheme' (taking its name from Matthew 9:38, sometimes called 'the other Lord's prayer') or its FIEC equivalent, 'Prepared for Service'. These programs, which last for one or two years, have three aspects. They give new graduates (i) hands-on training in pastoral ministry; (ii) a program of guided theological study; and (iii) the chance to serve in practical ways to lighten the load on the church staff. Apprentices have much to offer in ministry and can multiply the number of hands available for parish outreach, children's work etc. But just as vitally, this is a time for the church family to invest in them. They will become the next generation of pastors and missionaries. [30]

Planning for opening events

1. Thanking the work force

An invitation to lunch or to an evening event for all those who have worked to bring dreams to fulfilment, together with their families, can be greatly appreciated, and particularly memorable. Few see the

29 Marilynn Sowerby also cooked for the speakers and stewards at the Keswick Convention, assisted by a team from other parts of the UK who returned year after year, surely a tribute to her team leadership skills. Marilynn is one of those to whom this book is dedicated. She joined the great cloud of witnesses shortly before Easter 2007.

30 For further information on apprenticeships see www.ninethirtyeight.org and www.fiec.org.uk.

end-product of their labours as they move on to other jobs once their own specific skills are no longer necessary. Following a short prayer of thanks for the skills God has given them to complete the task, the pastor can speak briefly, and perhaps give each person a book to take home as a gift. This is an evangelistic opportunity not to be missed.[31]

Some churches have held a 'thank you' event just for the workers on-site; others have broadened it to include the lawyers who helped with land purchase negotiations, the architects, surveyors, building contractors, and interior designers. Church by church will have had more or fewer within the church family itself able to bring the needed skills. Where the skills have been drawn in from the local town, an invitation like this will not be forgotten.[32] Depending on the sympathy of civic leaders, it could be good to invite them either to the 'thank you' event, or to the opening service.

2. Celebration Praise

This is what everyone has been looking forward to. It is a time for thanksgiving which may double with the first service in the new building; or could be held midweek and then shared with leaders or representatives of other churches in the area.

The Thanksgiving Service in Dewsbury attracted a good number of friends and visitors. Graham Heaps, who had been pastor for 41 years and was due to retire at the end of the year, preached on Psalm 126. He spoke of how God had been at work throughout the project, and how that should give the church confidence to look to him for future blessing. The finished building was far beyond what most of the church family had imagined. It was indeed God's wonderful provision.

At the joyful formal opening in St John's, Carlisle, on 5 September

31 A small brochure with times of services and news of any courses the church runs for those who want to know more could be made available.

32 St John's Burford invited staff from the building firm and design team, and their families, to join the main Sunday morning service immediately prior to the commencement of building work. The service included specific prayer for the project, for its success and for safety.

2010, James Newcombe, Bishop of Carlisle, preached, and Steve Donald was able to include a time-lapse video.[33] The service was followed by a barbecue, recorded in the church register as 'breezy, but fun'. The register also records that 'there was a buzz about the place'. 'Breezy but fun' would sum up our experience of the building project', said Steve. 'Sometimes we felt like the disciples rowing against the wind but we also felt the exhilaration of throwing caution to the wind and trusting God.' He adds, 'the "buzz about the place" at the opening has lasted. Visitors speak of sensing God's presence at our Sunday service and opportunities to use the building for the community have multiplied.'

St John's now provides a large and flexible space under the original attractive beamed ceiling. The blue chairs sit on a light-beige carpet, and the glass entrance door streams the afternoon sun down the church to the east end. Tables and chairs towards the back of the church, near the main entrance, enable the space to double as a café area.

For Cornerstone Church, Nottingham the first Sunday in the new building had to be delayed by two weeks, as is not unknown for the handover of such projects. But this meant it clashed with the annual Nottingham Marathon—and the building wasn't accessible due to road closures! The leadership decided to have an afternoon service instead, and continued to have Sunday afternoon services on Marathon Sunday for a few years afterwards. These proved timely reminders of God's goodness to the church. 'That afternoon, the last Sunday in September, 2012', explains Paul Couchman, 'Peter Lewis preached from 1 Peter 2:6, reminding us that we are to be true to our name as a church: Christ is the Cornerstone on which we build.'

Here is the climax of much labour exerted over the years—the yearning, the prayer, the giving, the evening committee meetings after a long day's work. The end of that process has come, with the start of all that lies ahead.

At St Andrew's, Leyland, the Campaigners formed a Guard of Honour for the Bishop of Blackburn as he entered on an October Sunday

33 See 'Fit for Purpose' at www.stjohnscarlisle.plus.com for stills of before and after.

afternoon, to dedicate the refurbished building. The service opened with praise of Christ in the singing of the great Trinitarian hymn dating back to the 7th century:

Christ is made the sure foundation,
Christ the head and corner-stone;
Chosen of the Lord and precious,
Binding all the Church in one;
Holy Zion's help for ever,
And her confidence alone.

It is God who is at work in us to will and to work for his good pleasure. Anything we achieve has been through that work in us. The glory belongs to God and not to us. The service in Leyland closed with the hymn 'To God be the glory'. It was a hymn the church often sang through the project, and those same words are engraved on the bronze plaque commemorating his enabling of the Vision Builders, now mounted at eye-level on the south wall of the chancel.

A similar service was held in St Nicholas on a Sunday evening in late June. Richard Bewes, then Rector of All Souls, Langham Place, preached and the All Souls Orchestra came as well, joining forces with the St Nick's musicians.

On that summer's evening, with light streaming through the stained glass windows, the church looked wonderful. Many visitors and local dignitaries had come for the formal opening earlier in the week; now the church family was back home on its own. Richard Bewes turned to the New Testament, and the final chapter of Paul's letter to the Galatians.

An ancient building had been altered for the contemporary world; a medieval church for post-modernity. There was every reason to feel pleased, with all the real and subtle dangers of self-congratulation. The Apostle Paul knew human nature and he cast the right perspective as he looked away, to the cross of Christ.

'May I never boast, except in the cross of our Lord Jesus Christ, through which the world has been crucified to me and I to the

world.' *(Galatians 6:14)*

The words went to the heart of the gospel, with all its paradoxes of death and life, joy and pain. For all that had been achieved in human terms—by those who planned, those who gave money, and those who brought their practical skills—the Undercroft was nothing to boast about. But the cross of Christ was everything to boast about. It was, he said, the epicentre of the Christian faith and the great interpreter of life. By it, and only by it, could values be measured; it was the definer of all choices.

Handel's Hallelujah Chorus brought everyone to their feet. Here is the compelling truth to drive every church building project. The Lord Jesus, our crucified and risen Saviour, is King of kings and Lord of lords, and he shall reign for ever and ever.

Advice from a Church Architect

We asked Alistair Beckett, an experienced church architect, to offer his thoughts on preparing for a building project. How can the church and the architect best help each other? The following is his checklist.

Each project is different, and as unique as designing a new house for a particular family. The rooms required are often similar from church to church, but the priorities for usage can differ greatly. The starting point is the vision of the church family, and the development of spaces to facilitate the ministries that support that vision.

Creating a building committee

Carefully consider the make-up of the Building Committee, to balance those with technical and finance skills with others. For example consider including those who are natural communicators/points of contact in the church. (At the construction stage a smaller, technically-minded committee may be formed to liaise with the design team and contractor.)

Effective communication

Good communication and consultation can build faith as the church family journeys together. Consider how you want the project to be communicated, and how often. Include this in the Building Committee's brief to the architect. The Building Committee should set out a schedule for meetings, for design clinics (see below), presentations, drawings, models, 3D visualisations, etc. Ensure plenty of time is allowed for questions and discussion at all meetings. An agenda, circulated in advance, allows those attending to know what decisions are required to be taken.

Design clinics

We have found design clinics to be particularly effective. These are meetings to which the leaders of each user-group in the church is invited, to review the initial plans with members of the design team and representatives of the building committee. These give leaders an opportunity for one-to-one interaction with the designers. We find this process ensures that important details are picked up; and it reassures users that their voice is heard, bringing greater investment in the project. Some churches have used a questionnaire, sent out to groups in advance, to prepare for these clinics. A questionnaire has in turn enabled leadership teams for each of the user-groups to contribute at group-level. Such interaction at group level can raise questions and comments which are often invaluable. The questionnaire typically includes questions relating to spatial needs for meetings and events, projected number of participants, number of rooms required, furniture, storage, use of catering facilities etc.

Forming the brief

Consider how you want the building to 'feel' as well as its functional requirements. First impressions count. What do you want your buildings to communicate? New entrances should be easily identifiable and accessible. Reflect upon the journey into the building for first-time visitors, especially those who don't normally visit a church. For example, what of those arriving for a midweek pre-school group? Think of the needs of people with disabilities, and of older people. The experience of a first visit can determine whether people come back. What aspects would make the entrance more welcoming, accessible and not intimidating? Perhaps a bright, naturally-lit space with comfortable seating, which can be viewed from outside, giving a glimpse of the community within?

Consider the variety of spaces required. For example community and fellowship happen over cups of tea and coffee, which is why many churches are developing welcome areas and coffee bars. Think about the location and purpose of these spaces, and how they function and flow in relation to the other spaces. Could a servery double as a welcome desk for services and conferences? It could be open plan, or able to be secured behind a sliding hatch. Then it could be accessed through a door by groups in an adjoining area, when the welcome space is in use for other activities.

The primary function of an open space may be for a cup of tea or coffee before or after services. We have repeatedly seen how this space has encouraged more people to gather and build community within a congregation. But they can also be used for small services, parents and toddlers, youth meetings, wedding receptions, etc.

Other requirements should not be forgotten, like church family use for weddings, baptisms, funerals, etc. What of one-off events? Or outside use of the building? How would people-flow work for these uses? What about external vehicle movements?

When considering the brief, review the current room-booking schedule. Look at activities which might overlap, and the spaces required, (storage, access to coffee-making facilities or a kitchen). Perhaps a change of the time of some programmed activities may allow better use of facilities throughout the week.

Cost—Floor Area—Quality

These are three key factors. Most of us would like the biggest possible building of the highest quality for the lowest cost. This however is rarely achievable. When working with clients, we try to determine which of these is the most important factor, and then determine the extent of the other two factors. This helps when working from the initial wish-list to a deliverable brief.

We often ask clients to consider how small a building they can manage with. This may seem a strange request from an architect, however there are few other organisations which build large buildings for relatively-infrequent use. (We realise there are some churches where the buildings are heavily-used.) When we work with churches, we seek to be co-stewards of their resources and to assist them to maximise value. Much of this relates to decisions made at the design stage, refining the requirements and specifications, and achieving maximum flexibility of use. We often encourage clients to consider creating fewer rooms and spaces, each to be used for a variety of functions with suitable high-quality furniture. To achieve this the building circulation must be designed efficiently (ideally avoiding long corridors) to allow multiple uses of the building simultaneously. Generous storage areas would be needed, leading off the flexible-use spaces, to allow them to be cleared and reset quickly and easily for the next user. The choice of movable and easily re-arranged furniture is also important.

Exploring alternative solutions

Sometimes a building project isn't the only way forward. Perhaps instead there are existing spaces that could be better-utilised if they had better decor, furniture and lighting? Perhaps a space in another local church or community centre would serve as well; or a rented unit in a local shopping area have greater impact? Building is expensive and time-consuming. So it is worth considering alternatives as part of a cost/impact analysis or feasibility study. We have had clients decide to spend money on ministries rather than buildings, and defer projects until there was a greater demand.

Cost and VAT

Ensure that the implications of VAT (in particular VAT Note 708) on construction and professional fees has been factored in; and also the effect of inflation, if the work is likely to span a number of years. Life Cycle Costing may be worth considering. This is a process where the capital construction cost is considered alongside future costs during the lifetime of the building, i.e. energy costs, maintenance, replacement, etc.

Thinking sustainably

When designing new buildings, it is important to consider the reduction of energy usage from the outset. Therefore ensuring high insulation levels in the external envelope (walls, roof, windows), and the use of green materials (BRE Green Guide) are a good starting point. However, it's important to note that choosing multi-use flexibility of space over against additional construction will reduce the heating and lighting bills. Once energy demand has been minimized, suitable renewable energy sources that match the building demands can be considered. Consider a simple Building Management System (which can be run remotely on a laptop) that allows heating to be controlled in line with room use and bookings.

Youth Zone

If creating a youth zone, can this have its own door and identity? What catering facility would be needed? We have found that a well-designed youth zone will have other groups asking if they can use it too!

Getting the most out of kitchens

Church kitchens are often highly-functional spaces with harsh fluorescent lighting. The kitchen in our homes is often where the meaningful discussions occur. We encourage churches to re-think the kitchen space whilst retaining all the functional requirements. For example the option of softer lighting and a large central island unit with stools around it could create another meeting space for an adult small group. The island could hold the catering trolleys below which are used only for large events.

The role of church offices

When considering the needs for a church office, ask who it is for. Does it need a clearly-marked entrance door for use by church members or the wider community during the week? Or is it solely a back-of-house administration space? On a Sunday, or at midweek events, do you need an Information / Welcome Desk? These questions will help you allocate space and locate accordingly.

Think early of acoustics

Consider the acoustic requirements of each space alongside the audio-visual requirements. The quality and extent of the AV system can have a large cost-impact and should be factored into budgets. If considered as part of the overall design, the acoustics can be cost-effectively treated by introducing acoustic plasterboard and absorbent materials.

Signage and branding

Lastly, consider including a brand/signage exercise as part of the brief. Building signage is important when communicating to the public. It says graphically who you are and what you do. Working with your architect or a graphic designer will help you consider how your signage, stationary and website can project a consistent message.

Alistair Beckett, RIBA, Director: Hall Black Douglas Architects
Architects Specialising in Church and Community Building Design

The 'one anothers' in Scripture

The emphasis on church as people is brought out by the Lord Jesus, and by the Apostle Paul. As fellow Christians, we belong to one another; our faith is a corporate faith. We are told to encourage one another, counsel one another, love one another, bear one another's burdens. It may seem trivial to move from exhortations like that to the benefits of talking over coffee after the Sunday services, but in a truly practical and down-to-earth way, good meeting facilities help a congregation to be built into a 'church family'. Newcomers can be welcomed there, new friendships can start, and existing friendships grow. As Christians we are part of the Body of Christ. We need each other.

- **Mark 9: 50** *Be at peace with each other*
- **John 13: 34** *A new command I give to you: Love one another*
- **Romans 1:11,12** *I long to see you… that you and I may be mutually encouraged by each other's faith*
- **Romans 12:10** *Be devoted to one another in brotherly love. Honour one another above yourselves*
- **Romans 12: 16** *Live in harmony with one another*
- **Romans 13: 8** *Let no debt remain outstanding, except the continuing debt to love one another*
- **Romans 15: 7** *Accept one another, just as Christ accepted you*

- **Galatians 6: 2** *Carry each other's burdens, and in this way you will fulfil the law of Christ*
- **Ephesians 4: 32** *Be kind and compassionate to one another, forgiving each other, just as in Christ God forgave you*
- **Philippians 2: 1-4** *If you have any encouragement in being united with Christ… each of you should look not only to your own interests, but to the interests of others*
- **Colossians 3: 16** *Let the Word of Christ dwell in you richly as you teach and admonish one another with all wisdom*
- **Hebrews 3: 13** *Encourage one another daily, as long as it is called Today*
- **Hebrews 10: 24, 25** *Let us consider how we may spur one another on towards love and good deeds. Let us not give up meeting together, as some are in the habit of doing, but let us encourage one another*
- **1 Peter 4: 8, 9** *Above all, love each other deeply, because love covers over a multitude of sins. Offer hospitality to one another… Each one should use whatever gift he has received to serve others*

Lessons from Nehemiah

Nehemiah has been described as the book for those who want to achieve great things. The St Nicholas staff team preached through it twice over the course of Building for the Gospel, once on Sunday mornings, and once on Sunday evenings. It brought help for those at the sharp end, and for the whole church family. The emphasis throughout is of working together. In one chapter alone, as Nehemiah describes the position of people rebuilding the wall of Jerusalem, the words 'next to him' appear over 20 times. The detail of the record shows that each person's role was vital. No-one's contribution went unnoticed.

Nehemiah led God's people through a remarkable building programme in the sixth century BC, rebuilding a people as well as a city. This book—hidden away in the middle of the Old Testament—provides some key principles for any church in building for the gospel. These principles come in pairs—balancing one another.

- **Prayer and commitment.** While the project grew out of his prayers, Nehemiah was willing to be the answer to his prayers (Chapter 1). Hudson Taylor's son said of his father, 'He prayed about things as if everything depended upon the praying. But he worked also, as if everything depended on the working.'
- **Vision and planning.** Nehemiah was spurred on by a vision; at the same time he did his homework, researching, surveying the

situation, and making plans (Chapter 2).

- **Leader and members.** Nehemiah was a team-player and he involved all God's people in the project (Chapter 3).

- **Sword and spade.** There were enemies around who were out to stop the rebuilding. Some opposition came from outside and some from inside, as God's people began to grumble under the pressure of the project. But nothing would be allowed to stop the work going forward. So they took a sword in one hand and a spade in the other (Chapters 4-6).

- **Walls and people.** Rebuilding the walls was the prelude to rebuilding the people in a new commitment to their Lord (Chapters 7-13).

Selected titles written or edited by Julia Cameron

General titles

The Glory of the Cross: Exploring the meaning of the death of Christ by James Philip (Hendrickson Publishers / Lausanne Library, 2016). Short, profound and deeply perceptive.

The Grace of Giving: Ten principles of Christian Giving by John Stott (Hendrickson Publishers / Lausanne Library, 2016). Includes 'The Gift of Accountability' by Chris Wright.

The Reformation: What you need to know and why by Michael Reeves and John Stott (Monarch Books / Lausanne Library 2017). Pithy and stimulating. Looks forward as well as back.

Unique angles on John Stott's ministry

John Stott's Right Hand: The untold story of Frances Whitehead (Piquant, 2014). 'One of the greatest partnerships of the 20th century.' A story John Stott himself hoped would one day be told.

John Stott: Pastor, Leader & Friend: A man who embodied 'the spirit of Lausanne' (Lausanne Library 2012). Timeline and photographs. Tributes and insights from friends around the world.

Silhouettes and Skeletons: Charles Simeon of Cambridge (Didasko Publishing, 2013). Traces Simeon's colossal influence down two centuries into UCCF, IFES, Langham Partnership, and the Lausanne Movement. Includes concertina of silhouettes.

John Stott: The Humble Leader (Trailblazer series, Christian Focus Publications 2012). Short biography of John Stott to introduce children to 'Uncle John'. Features walking maps of Cambridge and London, Fact-files, and stories not published elsewhere.

/ continued over

Lausanne Movement

Christ our Reconciler: Gospel / Church / World (IVP / Lausanne Library, 2012). Formal published record of the Third Lausanne Congress. Some of the sharpest evangelical thinking on issues facing the global church.

Cape Town Commitment Study Edition by Rose Dowsett (Hendrickson Publishers / Lausanne Library, 2012) and *Cape Town Commitment Bibliographic Resources* compiled by Darrell Bock (Wipf and Stock / Lausanne Library, 2012).

The Lausanne Legacy: Landmarks in Global Mission (Hendrickson Publishers / Lausanne Library, 2016). Major outcomes of three Lausanne Congresses, with Closing Addresses. Foreword by Leighton Ford; Afterword by Michael Oh.

Further Recommended Reading

Christ and his people: Eight convictions about the local church by Mark Ashton (Christian Focus Publications, 2016).